Leckie✕Leckie
Scotland's leading educational publishers

SECOND EDITION 2

D0552069

STANDARD GRADE
Modern Studies

course notes **2nd edition**

Patrick Carson ✕ Irene Morrison

ISBN 978-1-84372-607-4

Published by
Leckie & Leckie Ltd, 3rd Floor, 4 Queen Street, Edinburgh EH2 1JE
Phone: 0131 220 6831   Fax: 0131 225 9987
enquiries@leckieandleckie.co.uk www.leckieandleckie.co.uk

Special thanks to
Project One Publishing Solutions (Project management and editing)
The Partnership Publishing Solutions (Design and page layout)
Eillustration (illustrations)

Printed in the UK by Nuffield Press

Acknowledgements
Leckie & Leckie has made every effort to trace all copyright holders.
If any have been inadvertently overlooked, we will be pleased to make the necessary arrangements.

We would like to thank the following for permission to reproduce their material:
Getty Images (pp 17, 18, 22, 24, 28, 42, 47, 60, 65, 69), Don Smetzer (p38), Mark Gilbert (p41), AFP/Getty Images (pp 43, 60, 71, 78), Congressional Quarterly/Getty Images (p54), AFP (p69), Guardian News & Media Ltd. (p88)

We would like to thank the following for permission to reproduce their copyright material without charge:
Bashir Ahmad (p35) Sabrina Maguire (p40), TeleFood (p87), FARM-Africa (p88) VETAID (p89) ActionAid (p89)

CONTENTS

INTRODUCTION

INTRODUCTION

Welcome to Leckie and Leckie's *Standard Grade Modern Studies Course Notes*. This book will be your invaluable study companion throughout your Modern Studies course.

The following pages contain advice on how to use this book and provide an excellent breakdown of the aspects of the Modern Studies Course.

But for now, enjoy your studies and good luck!

How to use this book

The Knowledge and Understanding section provides you with a structure for your study, covering each aspect of the course in a clear and concise way. Activities, case studies, guided research and 'hints and tips' have been specially designed to help structure your learning and prepare you for the exam.

Case studies and guided research

As well as providing some case studies, the book guides you in your independent research with questions and hints to focus your research.

Visit **www.leckieandleckie.co.uk** to find links to the websites mentioned in the book along with other related sites of interest. Either click on the **Learning Lab** option on the **Students** menu or navigate to Leckie and Leckie's Standard Grade Modern Studies Course Notes page and click on the **web links** icon.

Activities

The activities found in the 'For you to do' sections contain revision and memory techniques to help you remember crucial points in the exam.

Study hints and tips

Look for the 'Hints and Tips' icon throughout the book. Here you'll find helpful advice about what you need to study for the exam, common mistakes to avoid, common questions to prepare for, as well as some hints to help you perform to your best potential in the exam.

Enquiry Skills section

The Enquiry Skills section (pages 90–120) develops the skills you will need in this section of the exam. It provides you with tips on how to approach different types and questions, and guided answers to typical exam questions.

Mnemonics and revision techniques

Before you begin, make sure you read the section on revision techniques (pages 6–11). It will arm you will invaluable learning and memory skills to help you learn and retain the information you will need in the exam.

The Modern Studies Course explained

Syllabus areas

Syllabus area 1

Topics:
- Scottish Parliament
- UK Parliament
- Trade unions
- Pressure groups

Concepts:
- Rights and responsibilities: Citizens in UK have rights and with these come responsibilities.
- Representation: Who represents us? In Westminster? In Scottish Parliament? In local councils? In the workplace?
- Participation: Ways in which people take part in politics, trade unions, pressure groups.

Modern Studies – thinking it through.

Syllabus area 2

Topics:
- Elderly
- Employed/unemployed
- Families

Concepts:
- Need: What are the needs of the elderly, employed, families? Who meets these needs?
- Equality: Differences exist between groups of people in our society.
- Ideology: Ideas about how these needs are met, e.g. by the government.

Syllabus area 3

(Note: you may have studied USA or China. This book covers only the USA.)

Topic:
- USA

Concepts:
- Rights and responsibilities: Citizens in USA have rights and with these come responsibilities. You need to know specific USA examples.
- Participation: Ways in which people take part in politics and interest groups.
- Ideology: What are the ideas of the USA government?
- Equality: There are differences between groups in the USA e.g. African-Americans (blacks), whites, Hispanics.

Syllabus area 4

Topics:
- European Union
- NATO
- UN
- Politics of aid – examples from Africa

Concepts:
- Need: Main needs of people/countries in Africa. How are these needs met?
- Power: How do countries (in Europe) look after their own interests?

REVISION TECHNIQUES

Below are some ideas to help you revise and do well in your exams.

Group/paired revision sessions

One of the best ways to revise is with other pupils. The advantages include:

- company: to make the revision worthwhile and interesting and to reassure you that you are not the only person who feels the way you do.
- deadlines: to help you work to schedule. If you have agreed to meet up to discuss a topic, you are more likely to complete your work on time.
- discussion: to help you understand ideas by discussing them with a friend. Your friend may be able to explain something to help you understand it. Discussion also helps you remember points. People often remember discussions better than what they read or were told in class.
- less chance of missing out a crucial topic: talking the subject over with other pupils will help you identify any gaps. Often your friends can explain something in a way that is easier to understand than your teacher's explanation.

A group revision exercise

This activity is for a maximum of four people.

- Choose a topic for revision. Make sure the topic is one that you will be tested on in the exam. Try to make it a small topic, e.g. 'the voting system used to elect the Scottish Parliament'.
- Individually, brainstorm all you know about the topic. You can do this as a mind map.
- Now form pairs and compare your knowledge. (Look for things you have in common.) For example, you may both have written down that each voter gets two votes.
- Now as a group, compare your answers. Go over each point and make sure you all understand what you have written down. Use your class notes and textbook to check for accuracy.

- Learn some examples to go with as many of the points as possible. You may get more marks if you have up-to-date examples to back up what you say. For example, in the Scottish Parliament election in 2007, the Labour Party won 46 seats, which is four fewer than they won in the previous election and one fewer than the Scottish National Party, so the Labour Party's 46 seats was not enough to keep them in power.
- Work out ways to learn the examples, especially if they are statistics.
- Now using the headings and sub-headings from this revision guide, check to see if you have missed anything out from your brainstorm/mind map diagrams. If you have, divide up the topics you have missed among the group. Each person should take one topic and, using your books and notes, find out about that section. Write down some brief points.
- Now, get together again and teach each other about what you have found out. Take notes.
- If you are stuck on anything, make sure you ask your teacher.

Mnemonics

Mnemonics are systems and techniques that help you remember things. Using mnemonics can make revision a lot more fun. There are several different mnemonic techniques you can try, as outlined below.

Initial letters

The initial letter method is very useful for when you have to remember a list, especially if the list has to be in the correct order. For example, the political parties in order of number of MSPs in the Scottish Parliament are:

SNP, Labour, Conservatives, Liberal Democrats, Greens, Independents.

Take the first letter of each of the parties: S L C LD G I

Then add words beginning with the same letters to make an amusing or memorable sentence:

Some	Little	Children	Like Digesting	Green	Ink!
SNP	Labour	Conservatives	Liberal Democrats	Greens	Independents

To link the sentence with the political parties, imagine and visualise the people from the sentence sitting in the Scottish Parliament.

When you need to recall the information in an exam, write down the first letter of each word of the sentence. This will then help you recall the names of the political parties in order. It might sound tricky at first, but it really does work!

Remembering numbers

Figures and dates can be hard work to learn and recall. However, if you are able to commit some to memory you will improve your answers in the exam. Mnemonics can help you learn numbers in the correct sequence through using images.

First you give each number an image. You can make up your own images.

0	=	hero
1	=	bun
2	=	shoe
3	=	tree
4	=	door
5	=	hive
6	=	sticks
7	=	heaven
8	=	gate
9	=	line
10	=	pen
100	=	bread
1000	=	sand

You can then use these images to build up a picture that will fix the figures firmly in your mind. For example, the number of MSPs is 129: 1 = bun; 2 = shoe; 9 = line.

Create a picture in your mind of MSPs eating buns and then throwing a shoe over a line = 129.

Spider diagrams and mind maps

When we read most books, we read from left to right, top to bottom; the information is presented in a linear way. Information presented in this way is very familiar to us, but it is limited because it does not show clearly in a visual way how the information links together.

Spider (or spray) diagrams and mind maps are ways of presenting information which do show how different topics are linked. These diagrams are excellent ways to revise, as brain research suggests that we store and remember information by making connections between separate chunks of information.

Spider diagrams

Spider diagrams will be very familiar to you. They are simple and a good starting point for revising a topic.

For you to do

A spider diagram

- Draw a circle in the centre of a piece of paper.
- In the circle write the name of the topic you are going to study.
- Around the outside of the circle write the sub-topics that link to the main topic.
- Connect the sub-topics to the main circle using lines.

This will give you a good framework with which to identify the topics you need to revise.

Mind maps

A mind map is a spider diagram that contains information in the form of pictures and text. Mind maps are more powerful, more visual and more complex than spider diagrams.

For you to do

A mind map

- Take a large piece of paper, at least A4 size, or A3 if possible.
- In the centre of the paper write the name of the topic you are revising.
- Draw a circle, or if appropriate a simple picture, around the topic title.
- Each sub-topic should be represented by a word written along a curved line coming from the centre.
- These sub-topics should then be broken down again into smaller sub-topics and more branches added.
- Sub-topics that are connected may be joined together by adding more lines.
- Eventually you will end up with a complete overview of the topic showing how different parts are connected.

Mind maps can be made more interesting by trying out the following ideas.

- Divide the mind map into different zones, for example, advantages on one side and disadvantages on the other.
- Use up to four different colours to identify different strands, for example, green to show advantages and red to show disadvantages.
- Use symbols, diagrams and pictures instead of words to make your mind map more visual and therefore more memorable.

You can use mind maps in a number of ways.

- Before revising a topic, draw up a mind map and see how much you already remember.
- Draw up a mind map at the same time as revising your notes. This is a form of 'active revision' and will ensure that you concentrate when reading your notes.
- When you have finished revising, a topic draw up a mind map to test yourself without looking at any notes.

- Use mind maps in your exams to plan answers to knowledge and understanding questions. It will give you an overview of the question and ensure you include all the important detail.

Revision cards

Revision cards are a very popular and successful revision technique, and have a number of advantages.

- Revision cards force you to include only the main information.
- You can design your revision cards to reflect you way you learn best, e.g. in pictures, mind maps, bullet points, etc.
- Revision cards fit easily in pockets and can be used for valuable revision in 'dead time', e.g. waiting for a bus or train.
- Revision cards mean you do not have to read through your whole set of notes.
- Revision cards improve your confidence because you have something to show for your work.

Index cards sold in stationery shops make excellent revision cards.

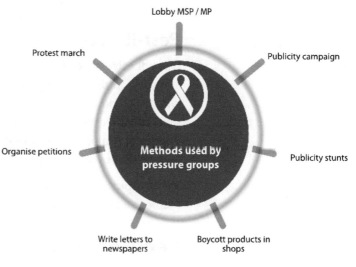

A simple spider (spray) diagram.

For you to do

Create a revision card

It is a good idea to design a standard format for your revision cards. This will make your revision easier to organise.

- Subject: write the name of the subject in the top left corner.
- Topic: write the name of the topic in the top right corner.
- Text: use key words to trigger recall. Break up the text using bullet points or numbers. Use a highlighter pen, or underlining, to emphasise the most important words.
- Arrows: use arrows to show how things link together. You could include small spider diagrams, mind maps or flow charts.
- Colour: write in up to four different colours. Be consistent, e.g. green for advantages and red for disadvantages. Using different colours will help your brain store and recall information.
- Maps: basic maps should be included for topics where locations are important.
- Cartoons: liven up your cards with cartoons to help fix the key points in your memory.
- Mnemonics: remember to include any useful mnemonics.

A set of revision cards.

Post-it notes

Use adhesive notes for bullet points, key phrases, important names and statistics on different topics. Stick them on your mirror, by the kettle or wherever you can see them to jog your memory. Some people associate different topics with different rooms (e.g. Elderly post-its in the bedroom, Politics of Aid post-its in the kitchen, etc.) and trigger their recall of the information by visualising where they placed their post-its around each room.

What topics or points do you think you should put on a post-it to help you to memorise and recall information? Note any ideas down now.

Revision tips and the brain

Short-term memory can only hold about seven items at a time. The information it holds, if not rehearsed immediately, will be forgotten in about 30 seconds. This is the 'in-tray' of the brain. To be remembered, information must be stored in our long-term memory. This can be stored, in any amount, for a lifetime. This is the 'filing cabinet' of the brain.

For you to do

Filing cabinet

● Draw your own filing cabinet with four drawers; one for each question (syllabus area) in the exam.
● Label each drawer like the diagram opposite.
● On the top of your filing cabinet draw three things that will help you revise, e.g. your favourite CD, chocolate or bottle of water.
● On the front of each drawer, make a bullet point list of the main sections you need to learn for that part of the exam, e.g. drawer 2: Elderly; health needs of elderly, housing needs of elderly, etc.

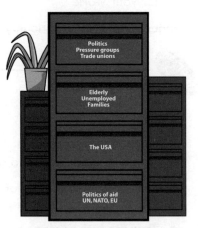

The filing cabinet approach.

Use this image to help you revise. When you are answering a knowledge and understanding question in Syllabus Area 2 on the elderly, visualise opening the second drawer and pulling out the file about, for example, how local government meets the housing needs of the elderly in your area. Once you have answered that question, put that file away.

What not to do

- **Never just read your notes.** Reading through your notes alone does not help you remember them. Exams are written, so you will need to revise how you will use the information in the exam. Use some of the written techniques outlined above.

- **Never leave revision until the last minute.** No matter how much you try, you will never revise everything the night before: this is impossible. Plan a timetable well in advance and reward yourself for achieving each target.

- **Never just revise the content.** Passing an exam is just as much about knowing the exam technique as it is the content knowledge. Remember to learn what the examiner will expect of you, e.g. how to answer particular questions in the correct way. Learn to use 'command words' correctly in the exam questions – they will guide you with your answer.

- **Never revise for long periods at a time without breaks.** Plan your revision periods to have regular breaks built in. Your brain cannot cope with long periods of intense revision – you have to take rests. Do not revise for periods longer than half an hour. Take a walk, or have a drink and then return to your work; you will remember much more that way.

Checklist of revision techniques

- Mind maps
- Spider diagrams
- Mnemonics
- Numbers
- Word association
- Group revision
- Speaking out loud (and put on MP3 player)
- Post-it notes
- Revision cards
- Filing cabinet
- Use the internet
- Listen to revision tapes
- Make bullet point notes
- Use diagrams
- Attend teacher-led revision lessons
- Revise in class without teacher input
- Revise in pairs
- Revise on your own
- Quizzes
- Library revision

In order to improve your performance in the exam:

- practise exam questions and papers
- analyse past papers to see what might come up
- analyse different types of questions, e.g. in enquiry skills questions the difference between a 'selective in the use of facts' question and a 'conclusions' question
- note the key words especially for knowledge and understanding questions, e.g. describe, explain.

QUESTION TYPES IN THE MODERN STUDIES EXAM

There are two types of question in the Modern Studies Standard Grade exam:

● knowledge and understanding (KU)
● enquiry skills (ES).

The following five chapters prepare you to answer knowledge and understanding questions and will provide a checklist for each syllabus area to guide your revision and help you practise answering knowledge and understanding questions. Section 2 will prepare you to answer enquiry skills questions.

ANSWERING KNOWLEDGE AND UNDERSTANDING QUESTIONS

The first (and most important) point to note is that to answer knowledge and understanding questions well you will need to do a great deal of studying. You will have to recall a lot of information and be able to explain it, giving examples to support it.

Point, Explain, Example, Concept (PEEC)

The examiner will look for certain things in your answers to knowledge and understanding questions, such as how detailed your answers are, whether you refer to the concepts and whether you have given appropriate examples to support your answers. A good way to make sure that your answers do all of these things is to 'PEEC':

● **Point:** tell the examiner what point you are making.
● **Explain:** go into a bit more detail.
● **Example:** give one or two examples to support your point.
● **Concept:** try to refer to the appropriate concept in your answer.

The PEEC principle.

HINTS & TIPS

The marks

The first thing you should look at in each question is how many marks it is worth. You will be awarded 2–3 marks for each well-made point. If you have made a very detailed, well-explained point, you can be awarded up to 3 marks. To be safe you should try to make at least three separate points in an 8-mark answer.

Imagine you are answering the following exam question:

'*Choose either the First Past the Post System or the Additional Member System. Explain the advantages or disadvantages of the system you have chosen.*'
(8 marks)

You choose to explain the advantages of the First Past the Post System, so your answer should be organised something like this:

- **Point 1:** The first advantage of the First Past the Post System (FPTP) is that it usually leads to strong, single-party government that represents (concept) the voters.
- **Explain:** This means that it is almost always the case that the government of the UK is made up of MPs from the same party and avoids coalitions. The party that becomes the government does not have to rely on the support of other parties in Parliament to get its policies and laws voted through so the government will be able to run the country more effectively.
- **Example:** For example, in the UK since the Second World War every government except one has been made up of MPs from a single party.

This is your first point. Now go on to make your second point:

- **Point 2:** Secondly, the FPTP system usually produces a strong opposition to keep a close eye on the government.
- **Explanation 2:** This means that …
- **Example 2:** For example …
- **Concept:** …

You can get up to 3 marks per well-made point, so in this 8-mark question you would need to make at least three points, explain each point and give examples to support each point. (N.B. For a 4 mark question you will need to make at least 2 points.)

Important things to remember

There are several important things to remember when answering a KU question.

Concepts

You do not have to mention the concept in every point in your answer but you must make sure you show the examiner that you know which concepts are involved in the question. For instance, in answering the exam question given earlier, it is likely that you would also make a point involving the concept of participation.

'Flags'

You should use certain words to 'flag up' or show the examiner what you are doing in your answer, for example:

- when you are explaining, you should say 'This means that …' or 'This is because…'
- when you are giving a supporting example say something like, 'A good example of this would be when …'
- when you have moved on to make your second or third point, say 'Secondly …' or 'Another way in which …'

Layout and structure

Make your answer look structured. Miss a line and start a new paragraph every time you start a new point so that the examiner sees three separate sections for an 8-mark answer.

This is my POINT in a concise sentence. Now I will elaborate on my point to EXPLAIN it more thoroughly. Finally, I will back up my point with some EXAMPLES to illustrate it. I should also mention the CONCEPTS involved in the question.

This is my POINT in a concise sentence. Now I will elaborate on my point to EXPLAIN it more thoroughly. Finally, I will back up my point with some EXAMPLES to illustrate it. I should also mention the CONCEPTS involved in the question.

THE DIFFERENCE BETWEEN GENERAL AND CREDIT

It is important to be very clear about the differences between KU questions at Credit Level and KU questions at General Level.

General Level

Every KU question is worth 4 marks. You will have about 5 minutes to answer each knowledge and understanding question. The questions will always ask you for two points, e.g. 'Give TWO reasons for …' or 'Describe TWO ways in which …'

Credit Level

The value of questions ranges from 4 to 8 marks. You will have just over 1 minute per mark. You will be expected to answer in more depth and detail than at General Level. Credit KU questions normally say, 'describe / explain, in detail…'

Types of question

There are two types of KU questions. Some ask you to **describe** … while others ask you to **explain**.

Describe questions: These ask you to show your knowledge and understanding of a topic and to write down that information. At General Level you will be asked to **describe two ways** … whereas at Credit Level the question will ask you to describe in detail … This means that you will need to **describe, in detail,** at least three things.

Explain questions: These ask you to give reasons and say why. At General Level, you will be asked to **give two reasons for …** . At Credit Level, the question will ask you to explain in detail, and you will need to **give three detailed reasons for …** .

USING THE KNOWLEDGE AND UNDERSTANDING SECTION OF THIS BOOK

Now that you have been shown how to tackle knowledge and understanding questions, you should use Section 1 of this book to practise this important part of the exam.

Be honest!

After each section you should ask yourself 'Did I really understand that?' If the answer is 'No!' take a note of the specific points you did not understand and revise them again. Ask your teacher for help.

Use the revision techniques

Pages 6–11 of the book show you some really effective ways to revise – make use of them! You are much more likely to remember information you have 'done something to' like make it into a mind map or a revision card.

Research your own examples

There is not enough room in this revision guide to provide examples for every point. The more recent the examples the better. Watch the news, read a newspaper or use the internet; the BBC and other news organisations often have search facilities which will give you access to a very large number of specific examples to support your points.

Use the Course Notes to structure your revision

If you follow the structure of the Course Notes you are less likely to 'jump about' in your revision. Concentrate on one Syllabus Area at a time and again, be honest! Don't leave the bits you found difficult to the end. Tackle them head on.

HINTS & TIPS

Avoid list-type answers

Although sections of this revision guide make use of bullet pointed lists you must not do this in the exam. Candidates who give list type answers will not score highly.

You should always remember to answer in sentences and paragraphs.

SYLLABUS AREA 1:
Living in a democracy – The UK

THE SYLLABUS AREA EXPLAINED

In syllabus area 1 you will be expected to show the examiner that you have a clear understanding of the following concepts:

- participation
- representation
- rights and responsibilities.

Areas you can expect to be examined on in this syllabus area are:

1   **The ways candidates are chosen / elected to be representatives in:**
    - the Scottish Parliament
    - the UK Parliament
    - local councils
    - the workplace.
2   **The ways representatives work on behalf of the people they represent.**
3   **How individuals or groups can influence or participate in decisions made at the local and national level or in the workplace:**
    - by voting
    - as members of political parties
    - as members of pressure groups
    - as members of trade unions.
4   **The rights and responsibilities of people and groups participating in a democracy.**

Referring to concepts

The exam tests your understanding of concepts. The concepts will normally be clearly indicated with bold typeface in the questions.

For example *'Explain in detail why women are under-represented in the House of Commons'.*

You should make sure that each answer contains references to the concepts, for example, 'Women are under-represented in the House of Commons for a number of reasons. Firstly, …'

WHAT IS A DEMOCRACY?

A democracy is a country governed by its people, usually through elected **representatives**. Democracy allows people to **participate** in important decisions affecting their lives. In a democracy the people have certain **rights** that cannot be taken away as well as certain **responsibilities** or duties to society.

Other features of a democracy include:

- regular elections
- a choice of political parties
- freedom of speech including a free media.

The UK is a democracy or, to be more specific, the UK is a **representative democracy**. This means that the people choose or elect representatives who will put forward the views of the people of the area they represent.

Participating in a democracy can involve more than voting. People are participating whenever they try to influence things around them, e.g. in their workplace, in the local community, in the nation as a whole or even in Europe and in international affairs.

Voting

Scottish citizens can elect representatives to various decision-making bodies. They can elect workplace representatives (shop stewards), local councillors, Members of the Scottish Parliament (MSPs), Members of the UK Parliament (MPs) and Members of the European Parliament (MEPs). The elections are held at regular intervals.

Joining and being active in organisations

Another way to influence decision making is to become a member of an organisation such as a trade union, a political party or a pressure group. Just as individuals have certain rights to participate, so do organisations, as long as they remain within the law.

Taking direct action

The right to take direct action within the law is very important in a democracy. **Direct action** is a term used to describe action taken to directly influence decisions on a particular issue. Direct action includes activities such as protests, demonstrations, picketing, petitioning, striking or organising campaigns.

Lobbying elected representatives

It is also possible to influence the decisions of elected representatives by lobbying them. Individuals or groups of people arrange meetings with their representatives to try to persuade them to do something or, indeed, stop doing something.

Voting in political elections is a very important way for people to participate in the running of their country in a democracy.

FACT

Referring to concepts

Responsibilities in a democracy

Along with the rights in a democracy, people should also:

- use their vote in an informed way
- participate in other ways such as those outlined above
- act peacefully and within the law when doing so.

For you to do

- In your own words, jot down what this syllabus area is about. You should mention the concepts as well as what you might get asked about in the exam.
- Draw up a table of the rights and responsibilities which people have in a democracy.

PARTICIPATION IN DEMOCRACY

Why is it important for people to use their vote in a democracy?

By voting, the people in a democracy let the government know how they feel about what it has done and is doing – or hasn't done. Elections allow people to peacefully replace their government. In non-democratic countries it sometimes takes a violent struggle or revolution to change a government or ruling power. If the government did not have to answer to the people on a regular basis, it may not act in the best interests of the people.

Although voting in the UK is not compulsory, people who have the **right** to vote also have a **responsibility** to use that vote. It could also be argued that people who do not vote do not really have the right to criticise the government if they do not like what the government does. One important reason to vote is that if a lot of people do not bother to vote, then this might allow extremist parties (who generally represent only a very small number of people) to be elected. Unfortunately, for some time now, fewer and fewer people are bothering to vote. In the last election for the Scottish Parliament, only 51.7% of the people entitled to vote actually did, although this was in fact better than the previous election in 2003 when the turnout was only 49.4%.

Why do people take 'direct action'?

Between elections, governments often need to make decisions on matters that were not issues in the previous election. The people have not had the chance to vote on these issues, so they may want to communicate their wishes to the government by using direct action. In other cases, long-standing problems may not have been raised as election issues, so people resort to direct action. The following case study is an example of people taking 'direct action'. Can you think of any other examples of direct action?

Direct action

Thirty-seven arrests were made after clashes between pro-Tibet protesters and police as the Olympic torch made its way through London. Protests over China's human rights record began soon after the relay began at Wembley, and prompted an increasing police presence through the city. One protester tried to snatch the torch from former Blue Peter host Konnie Huq. A contingent of pro-China supporters also tried to make their voices heard along the route, waving Chinese and Olympic flags and calling for 'one China'.

Outside Downing Street there were chaotic scenes as former Olympic heptathlon gold medallist Denise Lewis took the flame to Number 10. Gordon Brown greeted the torch outside Number 10 despite coming under pressure to boycott the parade and the Beijing Olympics opening ceremony. However, he did not hold it. Several small scuffles broke out as police tackled some of the protesters. Beijing Olympic torch relay spokesman Qu Yingpu told the BBC: 'This is not the right time, the right platform, for any people to voice their political views.'

Source: adapted from BBC News Front Page article, April 2008

For you to do

- Give three reasons why it is important for people in a democracy to use their vote.
- Do you think that the people involved in the pro-Tibet protests described above had the right to do as they did? Give reasons for your answer.
- Is there any evidence that the actions of the protestors had any effect?
- There are two points of view expressed in the article. Which do you agree with and why?

Internet research

In the exam you will be expected to illustrate the points you make in your answers by using recent examples. You can do this by looking through newspapers, watching the television news or by using the internet.
A good starting place is the BBC News Front Page website.

Organising your research notes

When you are researching, it is a good idea to structure your notes. Here is one possible way to organise your note taking. In this case it is for researching examples of direct action.

DIRECT ACTION RESEARCH	DETAILS OF DIRECT ACTION	WHAT WERE THEY AIMING TO ACHIEVE?	HOW SUCCESSFUL WERE THEY?
Example 1 (Source)			
Example 2 (Source)			
Example 3 (Source)			

PRESSURE GROUPS

What are pressure groups and how do they work?

A **pressure group** is an organisation of people who share similar views or goals. Pressure groups usually want to change something. They may put pressure on people or organisations, including the government, local authorities (the council), businesses and the media in order to influence their decisions.

Pressure groups can be small, local groups that may only exist for a short time, such as a group set up to save a school from closure. Larger international groups exist to change more than one thing, such as Greenpeace and CND (Campaign for Nuclear Disarmament).

Methods used by pressure groups

Pressure groups have the right to use a number of methods to try to influence decision makers including:

- lobbying elected representatives such as MSPs and local councillors
- publicity campaigns, e.g. posters, leaflets, advertisements in the press
- publicity stunts to attract media attention
- **boycotting** products, shops, companies, etc.
- writing letters, organising petitions
- protest marches and demonstrations
- convincing MPs, MSPs or Councillors to argue for their cause
- taking direct action.

Boycott: refuse to take part in, deal with or trade with a company or organisation.

A group which has been in the news recently is the Countryside Alliance. On their website, they describe themselves like this:

'The Countryside Alliance works for everyone who loves the countryside and the rural way of life. Through campaigning, lobbying, publicity and education the Alliance influences legislation and public policy that impacts on the countryside, rural people and their activities.'

Internet research

- Visit the website of the Countryside Alliance, and then search some news websites for articles about this group.
- What kinds of issues are they concerned with?
- What kind of actions have they taken?

Some other groups you may wish to research are:

- Greenpeace
- CND
- GM-Free Scotland.

Try to find out about a local group in your area – look in the local newspapers or online.

For you to do

Try these questions in exam time limits. You should take no more than 10 minutes for each.

- Apart from voting, in what ways can people participate in a democracy?
- Describe, in detail, the rights and responsibilities people have in a democracy.
- Make a spider diagram showing the main features of a representative democracy.

Rights and responsibilities of pressure groups

Pressure groups are like any other organisation or individual in a democracy; they have the right to participate in all of the ways outlined above. They have the right to organise and meet peacefully without harassment and have the protection of the law. Pressure groups are entitled to freedom of speech and are allowed to raise funds.

Pressure groups also have the responsibility to obey the law and use only peaceful methods. They must keep accounts for any money they may collect and they must represent the views of the majority of their members.

For you to do

- What are pressure groups?
- Make a mind map of the sort of actions that can be taken be pressure groups.
- In what ways are pressure groups similar to individuals in a democracy?

Beating the clock!

The most common complaint made by students during exams is that they run out of time. Keep a close eye on the clock. At Credit Level, allow 30 minutes for each syllabus area. In the Credit Paper you have just over 1 minute per mark.

In the General Paper you have just over 20 minutes for each syllabus area.

Practise answering 4-, 6- and 8-mark versions of the same question in exam time to see how much you can write in the time available.

TRADE UNIONS

What are trade unions?

A trade union is an organisation of workers that tries to protect and improve the working conditions of its members. Trade unions also represent the views of workers to management and employers. It works like this:

- the union members in the workplace elect a representative (shop steward)
- the shop steward negotiates with the management to try to solve any disputes between management and workers
- the shop steward passes on the views of his/her members to the people who run the union
- the shop steward explains union policies to his/her members.

HINTS & TIPS

> Trade unions are a kind of pressure group, so remember that they have the same rights and responsibilities as pressure groups as well as those on the opposite page.

Why do some workers join a union?

In a democracy people can choose whether to join a trade union. Unions represent workers to negotiate for improved wages and conditions meaning that individual workers do not have to negotiate alone. Unions can prevent individual members from being victimised by their employer. They can also make sure workers get their entitlements, such as breaks, minimum pay, holiday leave and that safety requirements are met. In other words, they try to protect the interests of their members.

Why do some people choose not to join a union?

In the UK there are about 7.3 million union members out of a total workforce of nearly 26 million. Workers may not feel they need to join a union if they already have good wages and working conditions. Some workers do not believe in the idea of unions or may not wish to take industrial action (e.g. strikes). Some workplaces may discourage union membership and not all trades/professions have a union.

What actions can trade unions take?

Most **industrial disputes** are settled before they get to the stage of industrial action. However, a union can take **industrial action** on behalf of its members in a number of ways including:

- **strikes:** workers stop working for a period of time
- **work to contract:** workers carry out no duties other than those in their employment contracts
- **overtime ban:** workers work only the agreed number of hours.

Grangemouth oil refinery dispute

In April 2008, members of the UNITE trade union working at the Grangemouth oil refinery, called a 48-hour strike, which led to the temporary closure of the Forties North Sea oil pipeline. The dispute with the owners of the plant, Ineos, over pensions was the first at any refinery in the UK for 73 years and caused brief panic buying of petrol and long queues at many petrol stations.

WORD BANK

Industrial dispute: a disagreement between employers and workers over an issue such as pay, working hours or safety.
Industrial action: protest action, such as striking.

Are trade unions effective?

'In unionised workplaces, occupational pensions are six times more likely and the provision of sick pay above the statutory minimum three times more likely (compared to non-unionised workplaces). Unions also reduce workplace accidents by a quarter.'

Source: **The Guardian, 6 January 2002**

What rights and responsibilities do trade unions and their members have?

Members of unions have **rights**, including the right to:

- elect the people who run the union, e.g. shop stewards or full-time union officials, such as the union President or General Secretary
- stand for election to the above posts
- attend union meetings and express their opinions.

They also have the **responsibility** to:

- take part in ballots for electing officials or deciding on industrial action
- act peacefully and within the law if taking industrial action
- accept the views of the majority in ballots.

Trade unions (like pressure groups) also have the **right** to:

- take part in industrial action if they ballot their members
- peacefully picket outside their own place of work
- operate in any workplace where the majority of the workforce want one.

Trade unions have the **responsibility** to:

- hold elections for important posts in the union
- obey the law when taking industrial action
- allow people to refuse to join or to leave the union if they wish.

For you to do

- What is the difference between a trade union and a pressure group?
- Either describe the role of a shop steward in a trade union or draw a flow chart diagram showing the role of the shop steward.
- Give arguments for and against the following point of view:
  'Key workers, such as those involved in the Grangemouth dispute or the emergency services such as police and fire-fighters, should not have the right to take industrial action.'
- Complete the following table:

REASONS FOR JOINING A TRADE UNION	REASONS AGAINST JOINING A TRADE UNION

- Allow yourself 10 minutes to answer the following question (which would be awarded 8 marks in an exam):
  'Describe, **in detail**, the rights which trade union members have when participating in the activities of their trade union.'

ELECTION CAMPAIGNS

What happens during an election campaign?

An election campaign is the organised attempt by a political party to win as many votes as possible in upcoming election. The party conducts a wide range of campaign activities at national and local levels.

The national campaign

At the national level, parties campaign using a number of methods including **party election broadcasts**. These are short programmes that often use advertising techniques, such as slogans, to win voters. Politicians may also appear on political talk shows such as *Newsnight* and will often tour the country in their campaign 'battlebus', travelling to as many **constituencies** as possible, especially those where they have a chance of gaining a seat. Most political parties are now also using the internet as a means of getting their policies across to the public. Almost all political parties have their own websites and some are using blogs and podcasts in an attempt to attract younger voters. For example, David Cameron, the Conservative leader, was the first high-profile politician to use podcasting in 2006 when he used the daily podcast service of the *Daily Telegraph* to talk about his party's policies.

WORD BANK

Constituency: A voting area that is represented by an MP (or MSP).

The local campaign

Locally, members of a political party can participate in the campaign by:

- organising public meetings
- **canvassing** voters, i.e. visiting homes to persuade people to vote for their party
- putting up posters or handing out leaflets
- travelling in loudspeaker vans
- contributing to campaign funds or organising activities to raise funds
- organising transport for elderly or disabled voters to get to the polling station
- voting for their party when the election comes.

HINTS & TIPS

Key words

As you revise a section, such as the features of an election campaign, pick out one key word, for example 'meeting' or 'canvassing', from each feature. In this way you end up with a list of words. You can then use some of the methods described on pages 6–11 to help you memorise them.

Groups such as pensioners will campaign at elections to make sure political parties produce the right policies to meet their needs.

The role of the mass media in political campaigns

One of the main features of an election campaign is its coverage in the mass media – television, radio and newspapers. The media plays a significant part in the election because it is the main way people get information about politics.

The broadcast media

By law, the broadcast media (radio and TV) have the responsibility to be unbiased in politics. It is from radio and television that the majority of people get most of their information about politics so it is important, in a democracy, that the broadcast media are unbiased. They are expected to give fair coverage to each political party in the form of party political broadcasts, news programmes, and analysis and discussion programmes such as Question Time and Newsnight.

The print media

Newspapers (or the press) are privately owned (Rupert Murdoch's News Corporation, for example) and have the right to support one party or another, usually giving biased viewpoints. They do, however, have the responsibility to keep within the laws of the country with regard to such things as libel laws or the Official Secrets Act. In other words, they cannot print lies or anything that would threaten the security of the nation. However, there is still some doubt about just how influential newspapers actually are. Research shows that many people will buy and read a newspaper which supports a political party which significant numbers of its readers don't vote for.

> **HINTS & TIPS**
>
> Get into the habit of reading newspapers critically. Look out for examples of bias in the papers. Memorise a few instances of political bias in a newspaper. You may be able to use them as examples to illustrate the role of the print media in politics.

For you to do

- Describe the part played by the mass media in an election campaign.
- What is the difference between the way the broadcast media and the print media may report political issues?
- In your opinion should newspapers be controlled in the same way as TV and radio when reporting on politics and elections? Give reasons for your answer.

VOTING SYSTEMS IN THE UK

In the UK four voting systems are used to elect representatives.

- Local councillors in England and Wales and Westminster (House of Commons) MPs are elected using the Simple Majority or **First Past the Post** (FPTP) system.
- The Scottish Parliament uses a mixture of FPTP and Regional Party List system called the **Additional Member System** (AMS).
- Local councils in Scotland (from 2007) are elected by a system called the **Single Transferable Vote** (STV).
- Elections to the European Parliament use the **Regional List System**.

HINTS & TIPS

In the exam you might be asked about:

- the voting system used for electing MPs to the House of Commons
- the voting system used to elect MSPs to the Scottish Parliament
- the advantages and disadvantages of voting systems including those which use proportional representation (see pages 28–29).

First Past the Post

HINTS & TIPS

It is very important that you do not make the common mistake of saying the party with the most votes wins the election. This is hardly ever the case.

The UK is divided into 646 **constituencies** (also called **seats**) of roughly equal population. Each constituency elects one MP to represent it in the House of Commons. The candidate with a 'simple majority' of the votes (even if it is only one vote more than their nearest rival) wins the constituency. The party that wins the most seats (not the most votes overall) becomes the Government. The second biggest party becomes the official Opposition.

Advantages of the FPTP system

- It is easy for voters to understand, resulting in fewer mistakes on ballot papers.
- It usually results in a strong government – one that does not have to rely on the backing of other parties in the House of Commons to get its laws passed.
- It usually produces a strong Opposition to keep a close eye on the Government to make sure it honours its promises.
- It keeps a close link between the MP and his/her constituency.
- **Coalition** governments (made up of more than one party) are usually avoided. Some coalition governments work very well, but others do not. Sometimes coalitions can be weak and unstable if the different governing

parties disagree over particular issues and then call frequent elections to try to win as a single party.

> **Coalition:** An alliance of more than one political party to gain the majority of seats in parliament and form the government.

Disadvantages of the FPTP system

- It can be unfair to smaller parties (e.g. Liberal Democrats) who do not get a share of the seats equal to the share of the votes they get.

- It can put people off voting for smaller parties or for parties which are unlikely to win particular seats. For example, a Conservative supporter who lives in a safe Labour seat might think 'My party won't win anyway, so why bother to vote at all?'

- A government with a large majority of seats in the Commons can ignore the views of the smaller parties even though millions of people voted for these parties. (This is sometimes called the 'tyranny of the majority.')

- Most winning candidates gain less than half the votes cast in the constituency.

- Most governments (even those that win in a landslide) win elections with less than half of all the votes cast. For example, in 1997 Labour won a huge majority of the seats in the House of Commons; they won 167 more seats than all of the other parties put together, and yet they only got 40.7% of the votes cast.

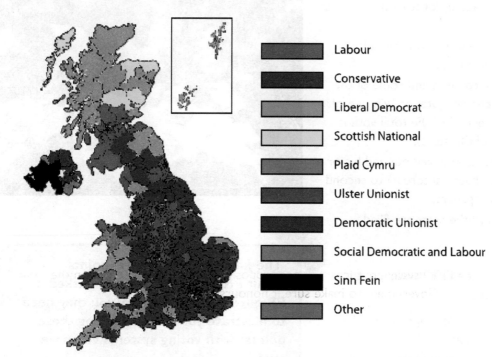

Labour

Conservative

Liberal Democrat

Scottish National

Plaid Cymru

Ulster Unionist

Democratic Unionist

Social Democratic and Labour

Sinn Fein

Other

A map of the UK constituencies, showing which parties won each seat in the 2005 General Election.

Proportional Representation

Proportional Representation (PR) is the name given to many different types of voting systems that try to share out seats in proportion to votes received.

> **PR is a 'group name', it is not the name of a particular voting system. In the exam you might, however, be expected to answer a question on PR, giving specific examples from systems you have studied. The Scottish Parliament voting system is a form of PR so you may use that as an example. It is called the Additional Member System (AMS).**

Some other PR systems are:

- the Single Transferable Vote
- the Alternative Vote
- the National or Regional Party List.

The Single Transferable Vote

- Constituencies are made up of several seats (not just one as in FPTP).
- The voter puts the candidates on the ballot paper in order of preference.
- The first choices are counted and some of the candidates will get enough votes to win one of the seats (a certain 'quota' of the total vote is needed to win one of the seats).
- The lowest candidate is knocked out and his or her votes are redistributed according to second choices on the voting papers.
- This continues until all the seats are filled.

The Alternative Vote

This system is similar to the FPTP system but is slightly more proportional.

- The voter marks their ballot paper with a first choice and a second choice.
- All the first choices are counted up for each constituency.

- If someone gets over half of the first choice votes, they win the constituency.
- If no one gets over half, the top two candidates remain.
- The remaining candidates have their votes shared out between the two top candidates according to the second choices on their ballot papers.
- This will produce a winning candidate.

The National or Regional Party List system

In this system the voter votes for the party they want to win.

- Before the election, the parties make up a list of candidates they want.
- The votes for the whole country (or region) are counted.
- Each party will gain the same percentage of seats in parliament as the percentage of votes it wins.
- If a party wins 50 seats, the top 50 names from its list of candidates will become MPs.
- This system is usually used along with another system, such as FPTP.

Counting the votes.

> **The following are general points about PR. However, if you are asked a PR question in the exam, you may need to illustrate your answer (using these points) with voting systems you have studied.**

Advantages and disadvantages of PR

Advantages of PR systems

- PR systems usually give a fairer share of seats to votes than FPTP.
- There is often a wider range of views represented in Parliament because governments are often made up of more than just one party (coalition governments).
- Voters are more prepared to vote for a smaller party knowing there is less chance of their vote being 'wasted'.

Disadvantages of PR systems

- PR systems can cause a 'hung parliament' in which a small party holds the balance of power between the two biggest parties. Small parties in this position are sometimes called 'king makers' because they hold the deciding vote in parliament meaning they have the final say in government decisions. Such small parties therefore can hold a disproportionate amount of power (i.e. compared with the actual percentage of votes cast for them).
- PR is more likely to create a coalition government. While this can be an advantage for the reason mentioned above, in some circumstances it can be a disadvantage. Coalition governments can be slow to act. They may have weak policies because the different parties in the coalition must agree before a decision or a policy can be made. Coalition governments can fall out and break up, resulting in frequent elections. Frequent elections are not good because governments do not have the chance to make many changes or look at long-term issues.
- Because MPs or MSPs are chosen by their party in some PR systems, the link between the constituency and the MP is weaker compared with the FPTP system where people vote for a particular MP.
- Some PR systems can be quite confusing for the voter. For example, the Scottish elections in 2007 for local councils and the Scottish Parliament involved both STV and AMS, and it is thought that 100,000 votes of the total of just over 2 million (about 5%) were 'spoiled' – i.e. couldn't be counted because they had been filled in incorrectly.

For you to do

- What is proportional representation?
- Make a key word list for two of the three PR systems explained above.
- Make either a list or a spider diagram of the advantages and disadvantages of PR.
- Explain the advantages and disadvantages of coalition governments.

THE SCOTTISH PARLIAMENT VOTING SYSTEM

The Additional Member System

The Scottish Parliament is elected using the **Additional Member System** (AMS). This is a combination of the FPTP and the Regional List System.

Of the 129 MSPs elected to the Scottish Parliament, 73 are Constituency MSPs elected by the FPTP system. The remaining 56 MSPs are elected using the Regional List System. All members of the Parliament, however they are elected, have the same **rights** and **responsibilities**.

Each voter at a Scottish Parliament election has two votes to elect two MSPs.

- The first vote uses the FPTP system. This elects the Constituency MSP.
- The second vote is for a political party (that lists its candidates), or for an independent candidate, within a larger electoral area called a Scottish Parliament region. This vote is cast using the **Regional List System**. This elects the List or Regional MSP.

The Regional List System

- Scotland is divided up into eight Scottish Parliament regions (based on European Parliament Constituencies).
- Each of the eight regions has seven seats in the Parliament (bringing the total number of list MSPs to 56).
- These seats are allocated according to the share of the vote each party gets in that region.
- Members elected to these additional seats are known as List or Regional MSPs.

Minority government: A government formed by the party with the most seats but which lacks an outright majority of seats.

Advantages and disadvantages of AMS

Advantages

- The Additional Member System reduces the 'disproportionality' of votes to seats often created by FPTP. This can be seen from the table of results from the 2003 Scottish elections. The Conservatives, the Green Party and the Scottish Socialist Party (SSP) won few or no Constituency (FPTP) seats but they each won a significant number of Regional (or List) seats.
- The FPTP seats retain the link between the MSPs and their constituencies.
- Parties can use their List MSPs to make up shortfalls in, for example, female or ethnic minority MSP numbers.
- It has created coalitions and **minority governments** which means that more than one point of view has to be taken into account when making policies and decisions, so achieving greater consensus or agreement.

Disadvantages

- List candidates are chosen by their party. Voters do not vote for individual candidates so the constituents might not know much about their List MSP.
- List MSPs do not have a constituency to represent. This has caused disagreements in the Scottish Parliament between List and Constituency MSPs about who should be doing what.
- The 2003 election led to a coalition between the Labour Party and the Liberal Democrats. Some question whether it is fair or democratic for the party that came fourth to have so much influence,
- The 2007 election saw an SNP minority government being elected. It needs to get other parties to support it in the Scottish Parliament to get its policies introduced.

30

SCOTTISH ELECTION RESULTS 2003			
Party	*Constituency*	*Regional/List*	*Total*
SNP	9	18	27
LAB	46	4	50
CON	3	15	18
LD	13	4	17
Green	0	7	7
SSP	0	6	6
Independent	2	2	4
SCOTTISH ELECTION RESULTS 2007			
Party	*Constituency*	*Regional/List*	*Total*
SNP	21	26	47
LAB	37	9	46
CON	4	13	17
LD	11	5	16
Green	0	2	2
SSP	0	0	0
Independent	0	1	1

For you to do

- Make a Point, Explain, Example, Concept (PEEC) plan for answering the following question: 'For either FPTP or the Additional Member System, describe the advantages of using this system to elect representatives.'

- Look at the table of the results of the 2003 and 2007 Scottish elections (above). Describe some of the major changes that took place between 2003 and 2007.

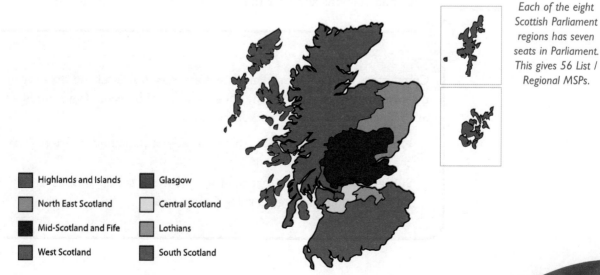

Each of the eight Scottish Parliament regions has seven seats in Parliament. This gives 56 List / Regional MSPs.

- Highlands and Islands
- North East Scotland
- Mid-Scotland and Fife
- West Scotland
- Glasgow
- Central Scotland
- Lothians
- South Scotland

REPRESENTATION INSIDE AND OUTSIDE PARLIAMENT

- Exam questions about how MSPs or MPs represent their constituents will often specify 'inside' or 'outside' of Parliament so pay close attention to the wording of the question.
- References should be made where possible to the Scottish Parliament unless the exam question specifically asks about the House of Commons.

How MPs and MSPs represent their constituents outside Parliament

MPs and MSPs can contact officials, councils, government departments, etc. on behalf of their constituents. They can join local pressure groups and campaigns to add 'weight' (importance) to an issue. MPs and MSPs can also use the media to draw attention to an issue or they could raise a matter with their party colleagues in local party group meetings to try to gain party support.

How MSPs represent their constituents inside the Scottish Parliament

MSPs can represent their constituents inside the Scottish Parliament by:

- asking a Parliamentary Question to Ministers and the First Minister
- initiating (starting) a debate in the Parliament
- introducing a Member's Bill
- writing to or meeting the relevant Minister about a particular issue.

MSPs can also take part in the work of committees that can:

- examine and suggest amendments (changes) to proposed laws known as Bills
- conduct inquiries and write reports for the Parliament to consider
- **scrutinise** Ministers and officials of the Scottish Government
- suggest a new Bill
- ask outside groups to present evidence to help the committee develop informed opinions and hear the views of a wide range of people.

Scrutinise: to examine carefully, in great detail; to ask questions to check honesty and accountability.

Scottish Parliament committees

Committees in the Scottish Parliament are very powerful and do a lot of the work of the Parliament. They are made up of between five and fifteen MSPs. There are two types of committees:

- **Mandatory committees,** such as the Audit Committee, are part of the 'rules' of the Parliament
- **Subject committees,** that the Parliament can set up, such as the Enterprise and Lifelong Learning Committee.

How MPs represent their constituents in the House of Commons

In the House of Commons the MP can represent his or her constituents by taking part in debates such as:

- adjournment debates in which individual MPs choose the subject
- general debates on the main issues of the day
- debates on the Budget
- emergency debates or urgent debates – these are debates called at short notice on a subject of a 'specific and important matter that should have urgent consideration' (as described on the House of Commons website)

MPs can also take part in committees of the House of Commons, which help to prepare new laws (Standing Committees) or examine the work of the government (Select Committees). MPs may question ministers during Question Time or the Prime Minister at Prime Minister's Questions. They can also propose Private Members Bills (ideas for new laws put forward to the Commons to pass and make into law).

How can constituents contact their MPs or MSPs?

Constituents can write to, email or telephone their MP or MSP at their constituency office. Constituents can also attend any surgeries held in the constituencies where the MPs or MSPs make themselves available. Constituents can also try to meet their MP or MSP at the Commons or Scottish Parliament.

What are the pressures on MPs and MSPs?

Why do MPs and MSPs sometimes have trouble trying to do what everyone wants of them? MPs and MSPs have to consider a number of different (often conflicting) pressures. They must, for example, consider what each of the following may want them to do:

- constituents
- the constituency party (party organisations in each constituency which select candidates, help at election time, raise funds etc.)
- party **whips**: each party in Parliament expects its MPs or MSPs to vote with the party
- their conscience: an MP's or MSP's religious or moral beliefs may not allow them to vote for or support certain issues, e.g. abortion or capital punishment
- pressure groups
- the national interest.

For you to do

- Allow yourself 10 minutes to answer the following question: 'In what ways can an MSP represent his/her constituents inside the Scottish Parliament?' Remember that specific examples are necessary.

- Why are committees so important in the Scottish Parliament?

- Make a list of the ways in which constituents can contact their MSP or MP.

- Visit the websites of the Scottish Parliament and the UK Parliament – both have very good sections for schools and learners.

Representation of women and minority groups

The 'typical' MP or MSP is white, male, middle-class, middle-aged and quite wealthy. Some groups have a much smaller percentage of representatives in the Commons or Scottish Parliament than their percentage of the population. For example:

- women make up about 52% of the voting population but only make up 19.6% of MPs in the House of Commons
- people of ethnic origin make up nearly 8% of the UK's population but in April 2008 they only accounted for 15 of the 646 MPs in the Commons (2.3%)
- other under-represented groups include working-class people and people with disabilities.

Why are women under-represented in Parliament?

- Political parties tend to choose fewer women candidates to stand in elections.
- Fewer women than men put themselves forward for election in the first place.
- The long hours and travelling that is often involved in being an MP or MSP can make the job difficult for those with family commitments.
- Many women are active in politics but often as members of pressure groups or campaign groups and not as members of political parties or candidates.
- As is the case for minorities, there is evidence to suggest that voter prejudice plays a part in the lower number of women elected as political representatives.

Female representatives 2007

ORGANISATION OR BODY	NUMBER OF WOMEN IN 2007	PROPORTION OF TOTAL (%)
House of Commons	126	19.6
Scottish Parliament	43	33.3
Welsh Assembly	28	22.7
UK Cabinet (October 2008)	5	20.8
Scottish Cabinet	6	33.3

Women in the Scottish Parliament

The Scottish Parliament works normal 'business' hours, making it easier for women with families to participate.

The holidays of the Scottish Parliament are around the same time as school holidays.

There is a crèche in the Scottish Parliament.

The Additional Member System has led to more women being elected.

Dawn Butler

Dawn Butler is the MP for Brent South. She is only the third black woman to be elected to the House of Commons. She states, 'I thought people in Parliament would be progressive. It is still a shock that they are not. Over the past 400-plus years, the only black people – and black women in particular – in Parliament have been there to cook and clean. For some politicians, it's still a shock to come face to face with a black women with any real power.'.

Why are ethnic groups under-represented in Parliament?

Fewer people from ethnic minorities attend private schools or Oxford and Cambridge Universities, where many of our MPs have traditionally been educated. There are also many voters who simply will not vote for a member of another racial or ethnic group.

Although certain areas have a relatively high percentage of minority groups living in them, the population of these groups is not high enough in most constituencies to get more of their members into Parliament. There are also very few ethnic role models in politics for young people to aspire to.

Scotland's first Asian MSP: Bashir Ahmad

Scotland's first Asian MSP has said he is 'very proud' to represent the people of Glasgow at Holyrood. Bashir Ahmad is one of four Scottish National Party MSPs on the Scottish Parliament's regional list for Glasgow. Mr Ahmad, one of the founder members of Asians for Independence, said he was getting his reward for years of hard work for that cause. He said that a school for the children of Muslim parents in Scotland was one of his main goals.

For you to do

- Describe the 'typical' MSP or MP.
- What evidence is there to show that women and minorities are under-represented in Scotland and the UK?
- Look at the reasons why women and minorities are under-represented. For both groups, list the four reasons you think are most significant.

LOCAL COUNCILS

Local councils are responsible for the provision of local services, including education, housing, social work, refuse collection, leisure and recreation. Each ward has a number of councillors who are elected using the

Single Transferrable Vote system (page 28).

In what ways can local councillors represent their constituents?

Councillors usually live in the ward they represent and so have a good knowledge of local issues. They can represent their constituents in many of the ways MPs and MSPs represent their constituents.

- They can contact officials in council departments on behalf of constituents.
- The business of the council is conducted through meetings of the full council or by smaller committees, such as the licensing committee. Councillors can represent their constituents through such committees.
- Councillors can draw the media's attention to an issue.
- They can gather the views of their ward by holding regular surgeries.
- They may attend local school boards or community councils.

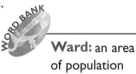

Ward: an area of population represented by a local councillor.

KNOWLEDGE AND UNDERSTANDING

SYLLABUS AREA 2:
Changing society – The UK

THE SYLLABUS AREA EXPLAINED

In this syllabus area you will be expected to show the examiner that you have a clear understanding of the following concepts:

● equality
● ideology
● need.

Areas you can expect to be examined on in this syllabus area are:

1 **The needs of the elderly, and the differences between them in the areas of:**
   ● wealth
   ● health
   ● care
   ● shelter.
2 **The needs of the unemployed in relation to work.**
3 **The differences in the wealth, status and life chances of families in relation to income and work.**
4 **How new technology can affect the wealth, status and life chances of people of working age.**

FACTORS AFFECTING WEALTH, HEALTH, STATUS AND LIFE CHANCES

How a person meets their needs can change as a result of different factors including:

● employment status
● family type (e.g. lone parent, two parents, extended family)
● growing old (some elderly people may have difficulty meeting some of their needs)
● income level
● social class; people in higher social classes are more likely to be able to meet their needs than people in lower social classes.

HINTS & TIPS

Avoid stereotyping all members of a particular group; not all elderly people or lone parents find it difficult to meet their own needs.

THE ELDERLY

The growing elderly population

The number of older people (aged 65 and over) continues to increase. Longer life expectancy means that more people will collect pensions for longer. What will this growth in the number of elderly people mean for the future and what problems will this cause **the state**? As the numbers of elderly increase, the working population (who pay taxes to pay for things like pensions, health care, education and transport) make up a decreasing proportion of the population. In the future it will be left to fewer and fewer people to pay more and more money in taxes to the government

Elderly population figures

- In the UK the number of older people (aged 65 and over) is growing and will continue to grow well into the next century.
- The proportion of older people is projected to increase from 16% in 2006 to 22% by 2031.
- By the year 2020, one third of the population will be of pensionable age.
- The 85+ age group is the fastest growing.
- There are more pensioners in Scotland than schoolchildren.

The state: a term used to describe local, Scottish and national (Westminster) government.

Older people (especially in the 85+ group) use more of the country's health care. The government will have to look at ways of raising more money (e.g. by making future generations of workers put more of their income into private pensions) to pay for the growing costs of services for the elderly population.

Why are some elderly people more able to meet their needs than others?

Some elderly people:

- are wealthier than others – they may have savings, a **private pension**, an occupational (or work) pension, as well as the **state pension**
- are healthier than others – only 3% of the elderly are in care (most can take care of themselves)
- live in better houses than others, e.g. housing with dampness can cause health problems
- have family and friends to help them
- know their entitlement to benefits and how to claim them.

State (age/retirement) pension: a regular payment made by the government to people over the official retirement age.
Private pension: a payment made by an investment fund to which a person or their employers contributed throughout their working life.

For you to do

Explain in detail why some elderly people might have much better lifestyles than others.

While you are not expected to give lots and lots of statistics in the exam, you will improve your answer by giving supporting evidence. Copy out and then try to memorise the facts in the 'fact box' about the growing numbers of elderly.

MEETING THE NEEDS OF THE ELDERLY

Who meets the needs of the elderly?

Most people over the age of 65 take care of their own needs. However, various groups and organisations give help to those people who need it. These include:

- the state (local, Scottish and national government)
- family and friends
- voluntary organisations and pressure groups
- the private sector
- technology providers.

How does the state meet the needs of the elderly?

National government meets elderly needs by providing:

- state retirement pensions
- welfare benefits such as income support, housing benefit, cold weather payments, invalidity benefit, attendance allowance, budgeting loans
- the National Health Service, which provides GPs, hospitals, prescriptions, health visitors, dentists, podiatrists, etc.
- free bus passes for travel throughout Scotland and free TV licences for the over-75s.

Local government (called Local Authorities in Scotland) provide a range of services to help meet the needs of elderly people living in their area. Services include social services, community care, council housing, sheltered housing, residential housing, nursing homes, home help, cheap or free bus fares and other price reductions. They also provide some benefits such as housing benefit and council tax benefit.

Free personal and social care in Scotland

In Scotland, elderly people can apply to their local authority for personal care, which according to their needs, might include assistance with the following:

- personal hygiene
- toileting, etc.
- food and diet
- problems with immobility
- simple treatments.

Medical care for the elderly.

For you to do

- Construct a spider diagram of the services provided to help the needs of the elderly by:
  - national government
  - local government.
- Which services are currently provided for elderly people in Scotland but are not yet available in other parts of the UK?

Internet research

Visit the website of the Department for Work and Pensions and take notes on some of the benefits available to the elderly and how they qualify for them.

It is very important in the exam to remember the differences between what is provided by local and national governments. (Scottish Government and Westminster) Do not make the common mistake of saying that, for example, the council provides hospitals; these are provided by national government.

Community care

Community care was introduced to provide care for the elderly (and other groups such as people with learning difficulties) in the community, rather than in 'homes' and other institutions such as geriatric and psychiatric wards in hospitals.

Under community care, elderly people are given a 'Needs Assessment' by the Social Work Department. This determines how well they can manage on their own and whether they can live in their own home or with their family. The sorts of services available under community care might include:

- accommodation in a sheltered house, residential home or nursing home
- home care services if living in their own home
- home helps
- adaptations to the home such as stair lifts, lever taps, ramps, walk-in baths, etc.
- meals
- recreational and occupational activities.

In addition, community care also provides support from:

- general practitioners (GPs)
- district nurses
- health visitors
- psychiatric nurses
- social services (e.g. care managers).

Advantages of community care

- By helping elderly people to live in the community, fewer of them need to live in institutions which are expensive to run and can lead to people becoming 'institutionalised'.
- It reduces 'bed blocking' in the NHS. In the past many elderly people stayed longer in hospital than they needed to because of a lack of suitable accommodation and services to send them home to.
- It meets the social needs of the elderly because they remain a part of the community and keep some independence.

Disadvantages of community care

- Sometimes the back-up services are not available because service providers are 'over-stretched'.
- Some people argued that it was a money-saving exercise, i.e. an excuse to close down homes caring for elderly people.
- The standard of care can vary a lot from area to area.

For you to do

- What are the aims of community care for the elderly?
- Which groups are involved in supporting the elderly in the community?
- List the advantages and disadvantages of community care. For each point you describe, decide on a key word, write down these key words and memorise them. Test your memory! Can you explain what each of these key words is about without looking at the book?

Voluntary groups and pressure groups

How do voluntary groups and pressure groups help meet the needs of the elderly?

Examples of such groups are:

- Help the Aged
- Age Concern
- Scottish Old Age Pensioners' Association.

Help the Aged and Age Concern help meet the needs of the elderly.

These groups can help to meet both the physical and social needs of the elderly in many ways, such as by providing lunch clubs and day centres. Some groups, such as the Women's Royal Voluntary Service (WRVS), run the 'Meals on Wheels' scheme. Groups such as Age Concern Scotland also act as pressure groups, bringing the issues affecting elderly people to the attention of politicians and others. Some groups provide important information and advice about complicated things like pensions, benefits and allowances.

Internet research

Visit the website of Age Concern Scotland.

- What are the aims of Age Concern Scotland?
- What services do they offer to help meet the needs of elderly people?

Family and friends

The family is one of the most important providers for the elderly. In fact, the majority of 'carers' for the elderly are members of their own family, most often a daughter or a granddaughter. According to the group Carers UK, there are around 6 million people providing unpaid care for their relatives and friends. Family and friends can provide a home (i.e. have elderly relatives live with them), help with money, provide personal care, and meet social and emotional needs by visiting, taking them out on trips, etc.

HINTS & TIPS

> It is important to remember that most people over 65 meet their own needs.

Many families help to meet the social needs of the elderly.

The private sector

The **private sector** also plays a part in meeting the needs of the elderly. There are many private companies which:

- run private care facilities (such as private hospitals, sheltered housing/residential homes)
- produce new technologies and medicines, e.g. stair lifts and other elderly needs
- may offer pensioners cash discounts (e.g. local hairdressers' pensioner days, bus company fare discounts)
- employ some elderly people because they find them hard working, polite to customers, trustworthy, an example to younger workers, etc.
- provide private pension schemes and savings and insurance schemes.

Technology

More and more devices are coming on the market to aid the elderly, for example:

- new medical treatments including drugs and operations
- stair lifts, bath lifts
- medical technology, such as digital hearing aids, pacemakers, hip replacements
- alarm systems (that help elderly people raise the alert for assistance if they have a fall)
- remote controls for many devices.

Sheltered housing, very sheltered housing, residential care homes and nursing homes

Almost all sheltered housing has:

- a 24-hour warden service
- flats for couples or single people
- facilities on the same level or lifts
- entry ramps for wheelchair access
- hand rails
- communal areas for socialising
- laundry facilities
- two-way intercom entry system
- help alarms throughout the property and personal alarms carried by the tenants
- adapted light switches, electric sockets, sink taps, etc. to make them easier to operate
- extra bedrooms so that visiting relatives can stay over.

'Very sheltered housing' for people who need more care provides the features listed above plus meals, help with housework and additional personal care.

Residential care homes are for those who require 'round the clock' care. They will also provide the kind of facilities found in sheltered accommodation but with 24-hour care. Nursing homes are similar to residential care homes but provide 24-hour nursing care.

Private sector: a term used to describe private companies and organisations (as opposed to state organisations).

Technology meeting the needs of the elderly.

 **For you to do**

Choose two of the following and describe, in detail, how they help to meet the needs of the elderly:

- friends and family
- voluntary groups and organisations
- the state
- the private sector.

THE UNEMPLOYED

In every country, no matter how well its economy is doing, there will always be people without work.

Reasons for unemployment in a country

Structural unemployment

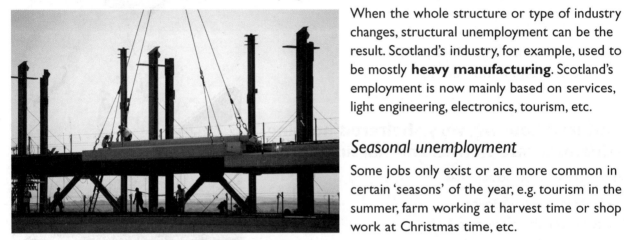

When the whole structure or type of industry changes, structural unemployment can be the result. Scotland's industry, for example, used to be mostly **heavy manufacturing**. Scotland's employment is now mainly based on services, light engineering, electronics, tourism, etc.

Seasonal unemployment

Some jobs only exist or are more common in certain 'seasons' of the year, e.g. tourism in the summer, farm working at harvest time or shop work at Christmas time, etc.

Labour-intensive heavy manufacturing.

Cyclical unemployment

Every economy goes through good and bad periods or 'boom' and 'bust' cycles. During a **recession** there will be higher unemployment.

Technological unemployment

When machines, robots or computers replace certain jobs, technological unemployment can be the result. The following are examples of this type of unemployment.

- Banking employs fewer people than it used to because of technology including ATMs (automatic teller machines – hole-in-the-wall cash dispensers), computerised record keeping, online and telephone banking, as well as 'smart' credit cards which automatically deduct money from accounts when used in shops.

- Newspapers and printing employ far fewer people than they used to because of the introduction of desk-top publishing to lay out the pages, electronic news gathering using the internet, satellite phones, etc. The printing process itself has also been computerised with the introduction of computer-controlled printing presses.

- Offices now employ fewer people in administrative roles because of the use of word processing, advanced copying machines, email and computerised salary and timekeeping programmes.

Heavy manufacturing: a term used to describe industry such as shipping, coal mining, steel textiles, engineering, etc. **Recession:** a period of general decline, part of the usual economic cycle; the 'bust' part of 'boom and bust'.

For you to do

- Describe the main causes of unemployment.
- In what ways has technology affected employment in:
  - banking
  - media
  - offices?

What are the advantages and disadvantages of new technology?

Advantages of new technology

- The cost of making certain goods is lower so they will be cheaper to sell and more jobs will be created as more people buy the products.
- The quality of goods will improve; computers and robots make fewer mistakes than people do.
- Boring, repetitive jobs can be done by machines, e.g. robotic car welding, spray-painting, etc.
- Dangerous jobs can be done by machines.
- Many people are able to work from home through computers using the internet, email, video conferencing, etc.
- Highly skilled (and so highly paid) jobs are created to design, build and operate new technology.
- Our lives are made easier, e.g. automatic washing machines, microwave ovens, dishwashers, etc.

Disadvantages of new technology

- Many jobs are lost as machines and computers replace people.
- Many jobs created (e.g. in Scotland) in the new industries are low-skill and low-pay assembling jobs.
- Many machines are almost maintenance-free, e.g. TVs, videos and washing machines, so repair workers will not be needed as much.
- Only those who can afford the new technology are able to benefit from it.
- Many of the hi-tech jobs in Scotland are created by multinational companies, e.g. IBM, Motorola,

Mitsubishi, etc. who tend to shut down their foreign branches in a world recession. They may also move to 'cheaper' areas, as with IBM switching jobs from Greenock to the Far East.

Car welding robot.

For you to do

- For each of the above bullet points explaining the advantages and disadvantages of new technology, decide on a key word, e.g. for the first advantage you might pick out 'cost' and for the first disadvantage you might pick out 'replace'.
- Make two lists of 'Good' and 'Bad' points of new technology, using only these key words.
- Try to memorise the key words using the techniques explained on pages 6–11.
- Recall the whole point from just the key words.

WHY DO SOME GROUPS FIND IT MORE DIFFICULT TO GET A JOB THAN OTHERS?

Some groups are more likely to be unemployed than others or find it harder to get a job. For example:

● older workers
● people with few qualifications
● women
● ethnic minorities
● lone parents.

Older workers

Employers may be less willing to take on older workers because they may need retraining, they may have 'out-of-date' skills, or they may be perceived as being more set in their ways and less likely to take instruction (especially from younger bosses). Older workers may need higher wages than young, single people because they may have family to support or a mortgage, etc. Many older workers will also have family ties to an area and so cannot be as flexible about where they work as younger, single people. There may also be employer prejudice, for instance, employers may think older workers are less fit than younger workers and are liable to take more days off.

FACT

Age discrimination in the workplace

In 2006 the Employment Equality (Age) Regulations Act was passed. According to this law:

● workers cannot be sacked for being too old or too young, as long as they are under 65
● workers have the right to request that they work beyond age 65
● employers have to give their staff six months notice of when they expect them to retire
● ageist recruiting practices are outlawed
● employers have to treat all workers equally when it comes to training, regardless of age.

People with few qualifications

Approximately 90% of the long-term unemployed have no qualifications. Because there is less traditional, heavy industry, there are now far fewer unskilled jobs available than there were in the past.

Women

Two-thirds of part-time, low-paid workers are women. Why is this?

- Many women work part-time and are not members of trade unions, so there is less job protection.
- Child care is still largely regarded as a woman's responsibility; it is expensive and sometimes is not available locally.
- Many women have career breaks to have children. This can make it difficult to resume their career at the same level before the career break.
- Employers may be against employing or promoting women with children, fearing they may take time off for family reasons.
- Most women still do most of the child rearing and domestic work so may not go for promotion because they cannot take on more work.

Ethnic minorities

The 2001 census showed that among ethnic minorities there were 2 million children (17.6% of all children) in households where there were no working adults. Among Muslim households (predominantly Pakistani and Bangladeshi families), the proportion was far higher. More than one third of these children are in families dependent on benefits. Reasons for this include:

- educational disadvantage – there is poorer schooling in areas of high ethnic population
- employer prejudice – the Equality and Human Rights Commission has shown that white people are successful 60% of the time they apply for a job but ethnic minorities are only successful 13% of the time
- culture – male Pakistani and Bangladeshi groups have proportionally higher unemployment rates than white British men, and more Pakistani and Bangladeshi women look after the home

- housing – Professor Muhammad Anwar, of Warwick University's Centre for Research into Ethnic Relations, has said 'unemployment is linked to bad housing. Bad housing leads to poorer health, and all these things are connected and have implications for each other.'

Lone parents

Lone parents often find it more difficult to secure well-paid jobs for the following reasons:

- working hours – lone parents may have to take jobs to fit in with the school day and with the school holidays
- travel – lone parents find it more difficult to take a job that involves a lot of travelling
- child care – this can be very expensive or it may not be available locally. The government only offers free nursery places to pre-school children; school-age children may still need childcare before or after school, so the cost may outweigh the benefit of working.

About 90% of lone parents are women – so many of the factors affecting women mentioned before also apply to many lone parents.

For you to do

Give three reasons why people in each of the following groups might find it harder to get a job than others:

- older workers
- people with few qualifications
- women
- ethnic minorities
- lone parents.

Where possible, make connections between different groups.

MEETING THE NEEDS OF THE UNEMPLOYED

The state and the unemployed

The state helps to meet the needs of the unemployed by:

- providing services such as the NHS (Scottish Government), housing (local councils), etc.
- helping them back into work through various schemes such as New Deal, Skillseekers and Modern Apprenticeships (Westminster)
- providing a range of benefits, such as Job Seekers Allowance (Westminster)
- providing Job Centres.

The New Deal

The 'New Deal' is a key part of what the government calls its 'Welfare to Work strategy', i.e. getting as many people as possible off state benefits and back into work.

All New Deal clients (unemployed people between the ages of 18 and 65) have an interview at the local job centre. A personal adviser is appointed to help each person on the New Deal. The interview establishes what skills and experiences the client has and what they lack. During the first four months (called the Gateway), the personal adviser tries to find permanent work for the client by:

- helping with job applications
- attending interviews
- drawing up an action plan to get back to work
- helping them draw up their CV
- improving skills through short courses.

If the person is still unemployed after the four-month Gateway period, he or she will be offered one of the following:

- subsidised work: the employer is paid a **subsidy**, and clients are paid the going rate for the job and receive skills training
- self employment: clients will be given help to

Subsidy: money granted to support an undertaking that is in the public interest, e.g. money paid to an employer to take on a long-term unemployed person.
Voluntary work: work (usually for a charity or non-profit organisation) a person volunteers to do for no pay.

start up their own business

- **voluntary work**: clients continue to be paid their benefits if they do voluntary work for up to six months
- the environment task force: clients take part in schemes to improve the environment such as energy conservation projects, etc.
- full-time education: if the client takes a course approved by the New Deal they will get an allowance equal to their Job Seekers Allowance (JSA) and any other benefits they are entitled to.

Schemes available to help young people

The main schemes available for young people are:

- Skillseekers (for those aged 16–24)
- Modern Apprenticeships (for those aged 16 and over)
- Educational Maintenance Allowance (for those aged 16–18).

Skillseekers is compulsory for young people who want to receive benefits. Training, normally lasting about two years, is provided by a range of organisations, including specialist training agencies, employers and local colleges. Each Skillseeker is paid an allowance. The scheme provides a mixture of skills training and on-the-job experience. It is intended that the training is of a nationally recognised standard, so that the young person gains qualifications and so is more employable. Some Skillseekers may be kept on by their employer at the end of their training period.

Modern Apprenticeships are aimed at school or college leavers. They aim to give the apprentices NVQ or SVQ qualifications. The apprentice is taken on by an employer and is paid either a wage or an allowance. These apprenticeships are available in over 80 different areas of industry. They offer the opportunity to train for jobs at craft, technician and management level.

The **Educational Maintenance Allowance** is a weekly payment paid directly to young people in S5 and S6 who qualify for it. It is aimed at helping them to stay on in school after S4 in order gain more qualifications and so help them go on to further study or into paid employment.

What benefits are available to the unemployed?

Job Seekers Allowance

Jobseekers Allowance (JSA) is the main benefit paid to the unemployed who are actively seeking work. The amount will vary according to the circumstances of the person, e.g. single, married with children, etc. People on JSA are entitled to free prescriptions, dental treatment and school meals. There are two types of JSA:

- contribution-based JSA is based on National Insurance contributions which the unemployed person has made in the past
- income-based JSA is based on the person's income and savings.

Sick pay and incapacity benefit

People who are not working due to illness may qualify for statutory sick pay or incapacity benefit.

Local authority benefits

Local councils also provide certain benefits, such as council tax benefit and housing benefit, to low-income earners and the unemployed to help people meet the cost of paying for their home.

Job Centre Plus

The aim of Job Centre Plus (JCP) is to help as many unemployed people of working age as possible to find jobs by:

- providing information about job vacancies
- providing advice, training and support
- encouraging employers to create job opportunities
- targeting help to those in disadvantaged groups and in areas of high unemployment.

The JCP also helps people work out which benefits they are entitled to.

For you to do

- Describe how the New Deal helps to get people off benefits and into work.
- Complete this table detailing schemes available to help young people.

NAME OF SCHEME	DETAILS
Modern Apprenticeships	
Skillseekers	
Educational Maintenance Allowance	

Internet research

Visit the New Deal website and make a list of the New Deal Programmes and who they are aimed at.

Job Centres help to meet the needs of the unemployed.

HOW DOES THE STATE ATTEMPT TO HELP AREAS OF HIGH UNEMPLOYMENT?

Schemes to help areas of high unemployment are called **Regional Assistance**. In Scotland, businesses can be helped by:

- Scottish Enterprise and Highlands and Islands Enterprise
- Scottish Development International
- Regional Selective Assistance.

Scottish Enterprise and Highlands and Islands Enterprise

The main aim of these organisations is to improve employment in Scotland. Scottish Enterprise consists of the overall national body (Scottish Enterprise) and a 'network' of 12 Local Enterprise Companies (LECs), each covering a specific area of the country. Highlands and Islands Enterprise does the same for the north and west of Scotland, including the islands.

Their aims are:

- to help existing businesses to get bigger
- to help new businesses start up
- to attract foreign investment to Scotland
- to improve the environment
- to improve the skills of the Scottish workforce.

They do this by giving grants and loans to new companies and providing expert advice to help people starting a business. They allow companies an exemption from paying certain taxes if they set up in a **blackspot area**. They may build factories for incoming employers and give a rent-free period to help them get going. They are also responsible for arranging training for workers in a particular skill needed by an employer and improving the local environment to make it more attractive to potential investors in the area (e.g. clearing up old, derelict factory sites).

Blackspot area: an area of high unemployment.

Scottish Development International

Scottish Development International (formerly 'Locate in Scotland') specifically tries to encourage foreign companies to come to Scotland. Many modern industries are 'footloose', that is, they can be situated anywhere because they are no longer tied to a raw material, (e.g. coal) as many of Scotland's older industries were.

Scottish Development International encourages these footloose industries such as micro-electronics, IT, etc. to locate in Scotland by:

- marketing ('selling') Scotland abroad as a good place for industry
- offering companies advice about what grants are available to investors (e.g. those from the European Union)
- giving advice about the best way to expand the business into the European Union
- providing incentives (grants, loans, etc.)
- providing advice to companies coming to Scotland about the best way to break into the US market.

Regional Selective Assistance

In Scotland there are designated areas called **Assisted Areas** where businesses can apply for grants to help them start up or grow. In these areas, businesses can apply for two types of grant:

- investment grants
- innovation grants.

The grants are mostly aimed at small or medium-sized enterprises (SMEs). These grants may be given to businesses so long as:

- they are located in one of the Assisted Areas
- they create new jobs or safeguard existing jobs
- they are financially viable
- they are mainly funded from the private sector
- they involve projects which represent a 'significant technological advance' (for innovation grants).

For you to do

Allow yourself 10 minutes to attempt this question: 'Describe, in detail, ways in which the state try to assist areas of high unemployment in Scotland?'
(8 marks)

THE FAMILY

Why do some families have a better lifestyle than others?

As with the elderly, there are many differences in the lifestyles of families and it would be wrong to stereotype them. For example, not every lone parent family is poor. The lifestyles of families will be different according to:

- income: some families have several 'wage earners' or may have very well-paid jobs while others may have no job and rely on state benefits
- health: poorer families tend to suffer more ill health than families who are better off
- housing: some families live in nice areas with plenty of space and amenities, etc. Others may live in run-down estates with poor quality housing, few amenities or high crime rates
- family size: families with more children have to spend more on food, clothes, etc.
- social class: studies have shown that families in higher social classes will have better lifestyles than those in lower classes
- family type: families with two or more adults in the house are likely to find things easier than lone-parent households.

Problems faced by some lone-parent families

Lone-parent families make up almost one in four of the families in the UK according to 'Gingerbread', the group for lone parents. Although not every lone-parent family has problems, it has been shown that they are more likely to:

- occupy poor quality housing
- live in rented or council accommodation
- live below the poverty line
- rely on state benefits (75% of lone-parent families rely on Income Support)
- be unemployed (in 2007, 51% of lone parents were in work whereas 72% of people living as couples were in work)
- work part-time
- be paid low wages.

How can the state help families and people on low incomes?

- Child benefit: an allowance available to all families bringing up children. It is not affected by income. It is paid for each child if the child is under 16. Older children may also qualify if, for example, they are in full-time education.

- Tax Credits: available to families if they are on a low or middle income and are responsible for bringing up one or more children under 16 years of age.
- Child Care Tax Credit: pays up to 80% of the cost of children being looked after by an approved childminder.
- Income Support: available to families on a low income, with savings of less than £16,000 and who are not working or are working fewer than 16 hours per week.
- Budgeting Loans (formerly Crisis Loans): interest-free loans that have to be paid back. They are available if a person or partner has been receiving JSA or Income Support for 26 weeks. Budgeting Loans are intended to spread the cost of things like buying furniture, household equipment, clothing or footwear.
- Housing benefit, council tax benefit and the New Deal are all measures that can help families. They are explained earlier in this chapter (see pages 46–47).

The National Minimum Wage

In Britain, employers must pay their workers a minimum amount – the National Minimum wage. For over-21s, the NMW was raised in October 2008 to £5.73 an hour. For 18-21s year olds the rate was raised to £4.77, and for 16-17 year olds, it was raised to £3.53.

What are the arguments for the National Minimum Wage?

- It makes it worthwhile for more people to find a job than stay on benefits.
- It helps the poorest sections of the workforce.
- It has not caused widespread job losses as feared by some.
- Other countries – including the USA – have them.
- It helps reduce the exploitation of young workers.

What are the arguments against the National Minimum Wage?

- Employers have to find the money from somewhere so they are forced to put up their prices.
- Some employers simply 'dodge' the law by not paying the NMW.
- Some employers get round the NMW by taking on 'casual' or even illegal workers. (There have been several stories in the news recently about employers hiring asylum seekers – who are not allowed to work officially in this country – and paying them very low wages.)
- Some employers replace workers when they reach 21 with younger workers so they don't have to pay the adult NMW.

For you to do

- Explain why some families enjoy a better lifestyle than others.
- What particular problems do some lone-parent families face?
- Make a summary diagram of the benefits provided by the state to help meet the needs of the family.
- Make a key word list of the arguments for and against the National Minimum Wage.

KNOWLEDGE AND UNDERSTANDING

SYLLABUS AREA 3:
Ideologies – The USA

THE SYLLABUS AREA EXPLAINED

In this syllabus area you will be expected to show the examiner that you have a clear understanding of the following concepts:

- equality
- ideology
- participation
- rights and responsibilities.

Areas you can expect to be examined on in this syllabus area are:

1 **The ideology of the USA:**
  - how the country is run
  - what rights and freedoms its people have
  - how the economy works.
2 **The different views within that ideology about:**
  - jobs
  - politics
  - human rights
  - what and how much the state should do to ensure equality in these areas.
3 **The ways in which the citizens of the USA can participate.**
4 **The extent to which US citizens actually do participate.**

WHAT IS THE MEANING OF 'IDEOLOGY'?

An **ideology** is a set of ideas or beliefs about how to run a country or, in fact, how to run the world.

Examples of ideologies that have influenced the world in recent times are:

- capitalism (e.g. in the USA and the UK)
- communism (e.g. in the former USSR and China)
- fascism (in the Second World War in Germany and Italy).

What are the main features of capitalism in the USA?

- **Privately owned business**: Most businesses, shops, farms and services in the USA are owned by private companies and not by the government. For example, Coca-Cola, McDonalds, airlines, power companies, etc.
- **The profit motive**: People set up businesses so they can make a profit. This is sometimes called the 'profit motive'.
- **Competition and choice**: A key idea of capitalism is that there should be lots of different businesses competing against one another for people's custom so the consumer will have lots of choices of goods and services.
- **The market system**: The price of things is decided by the market system, sometimes described as supply and demand, i.e. how many goods are for sale (supply) and how many people want them (demand).
- **Non-intervention**: The government in a capitalist country will not interfere too much in the running of the economy, leaving most of this up to private business, sometimes called **private enterprise**.

Why does the economy of the USA allow some Americans to have high living standards?

- They do well at school, college, university and gain good qualifications which lead to better jobs.
- They work hard to achieve the 'American dream' – by owning their own business and making profit.
- The USA is one of the richest countries in the world, so they have a better chance of having a good standard of living.

For you to do

Make a spider diagram of the main features of capitalism in the USA.

THE POLITICAL SYSTEM OF THE USA

Representative democracy

In the USA, the political system (how the government runs the country) is called a **representative democracy**. In a representative democracy such as the USA, all adults over a certain age (18 in the USA) have the right to vote, unless they are in prison or on probation, or have been judged by a court to be mentally incapable. There will be more than one political party to choose from in elections. In the USA, for example, the two main parties are the Republicans and the Democrats.

There are many elections for political positions. In a democracy such as the USA, the people are able to participate in the running of their country in many ways. They also have certain rights that are guaranteed and protected by the Constitution. The main way people participate is by voting. In the USA the people vote in lots of elections at different levels:

● local elections
● state elections (there are 50 different states)
● Federal elections for the President and Congress.

Internet research

Visit the websites of the Republican and Democratic parties. What issues are discussed? What are the differences between the policies of the two parties? (NB you may see the Republican Party referred to as 'GOP' meaning 'Grand Old Party'.)

What rights and responsibilities do US citizens have?

A recent demonstration in America.

In democracies such as the USA, citizens have certain rights, i.e. things they are free to do or are entitled to.

The rights of American citizens are set out in a series of Amendments to the Constitution called **The Bill of Rights** which guarantees the following rights (as well as others):

● the right to freedom of speech (the 1st Amendment)
● the right to carry guns (the 2nd Amendment)
● the right to vote (the 26th Amendment)
● the right of assembly.

Having rights also means having responsibilities. Here are some examples:

Right	Responsibility
To vote for a large number of elected posts at various levels of government	To use their vote, to accept the results of democratic election
To freedom of speech	To respect the views of others, to not commit libel or slander, to tell the truth
To protest, demonstrate and take other forms of direct action	To act peacefully and stay within the law
To join a political party or an interest group	To support these groups by for example, contributing money, taking part in their campaigns etc
To bear arms	To keep guns safe and secure, to use them only in self-defence
To freedom of the media – TV, newspapers, etc. can criticise the government	To respect the privacy of individuals, to tell the truth

Examples of political rights and responsibilities are given in the table below.

Right	Responsibility	Example
To stand for election	To run a fair campaign	Presidential campaign 2008, Obama vs McCain
To join a political party	To support the party ideology	Democratic vs Republican
To vote freely for chosen candidate	To accept result of election	Vote for Governor of a state
To protest against a law	To protest peacefully	Anti-abortion protests
To join an interest group	To protest peacefully	National Rifle Association

For you to do

- Why do you think it is important in a democracy for people to have the right to freedom of speech?
- In some countries voting is compulsory. Do you think this should be the case in the USA? Give reasons for your answer.

FACT

The First Amendment is a very important one as it is the basis of many important rights in the USA:

'*Congress shall make no law respecting an establishment of religion, or prohibiting the free exercise thereof; or abridging the freedom of speech, or of the press; or the right of the people peaceably to assemble, and to petition the Government for a redress of grievances.*'

THE CONSTITUTION OF THE USA

The **Constitution** of a country is the set of rules by which the country is run. The Constitution of the USA details such things as what powers the President shall have, what powers Congress and the judiciary have, etc.

How are the rights of US citizens protected by the Constitution?

The Bill of Rights is guaranteed by the Constitution. The Constitution is the highest law in the land, which means the rights laid out in the Bill of Rights are the law of the land. People can take legal action if they are denied their rights.

The people of the USA have the right to participate in the running of their country. They can take political action to protect their rights. The Supreme Court of the USA is the highest court in the USA. Its main job is to protect people's rights as laid down in the Constitution.

How US citizens can participate in the running of their country

People in a representative democracy like the USA can participate in the running of the country (or try to get things done or changed) in a number of ways including:

- voting in city, state and Federal elections for mayors, governors, members of the House of Representatives and senators, respectively
- joining interest groups, e.g. ACLU (see Fact box opposite)
- joining a political party such as the Democrats or the Republicans
- founding a political party or interest group
- standing as candidates in elections
- taking direct action, such as holding demonstrations, lobbying senators, making petitions or going on strike, e.g. Justice for Janitors
- using the media to get their point of view across, e.g. the *Washington Post*.

HINTS & TIPS

In previous years, Credit candidates have been asked to describe the 'political rights' of US citizens. The list showing how people can participate also describes their political rights.

HINTS & TIPS

Do not make the common mistake of giving UK examples to illustrate a US answer. For example, do not say that people can elect MPs; this is a very common mistake.

For you to do

Questions about the ways in which people in the USA can participate are common in the exam so you should be very familiar with this topic. Create a mind map called 'Participation' showing the ways in which people can participate in the USA. Make sure you use American examples.

Internet research

To see a text of the US Constitution go to the Constitution website (a link to this can be found on the Modern Studies links page on the Leckie and Leckie website). Note how short a document it is.

Interest groups

Joining an interest group can be a way for US citizens to participate in the running of their country. Some interest groups are very powerful and can even influence government policies. The following case study is an example of an interest group in the USA.

The American Civil Liberties Union (ACLU)

The American Civil Liberties Union (ACLU) is an American interest group. It works to defend and preserve the individual rights and liberties guaranteed to US citizens by the Constitution and laws of the United States.

Internet research

Go to the ACLU's website and complete the following.

- Briefly outline the four main areas of the 'mission of the ACLU' described on the home page.
- What methods does it use in its work?
- Which 'segments of the population' does the ACLU seek to extend rights to?
- Why do you think the ACLU believes it is important to let people know that they do not receive government funding?
- Take notes of some of the current campaigns and issues the ACLU is involved in.

Internet research

Using the internet, make brief notes on the aims of one or two of the interest groups mentioned below. Remember, the examiner will give high credit to well-exemplified answers.

- The American Federation of Labor / Congress of Industrial Organisations
- AARP – American Association for Retired Persons
- Center for American Women and Politics
- Coalition to Stop Gun Violence
- National Rifle Association (NRA)
- Veterans of Foreign Wars

THE POLITICAL SYSTEM IN THE USA

Separation of the powers

An important part of the Constitution is that the three main powers of government are given to three different parts or branches of the system. This is called 'Separation of the powers'. It is designed to stop any one branch of the system becoming too powerful. This separation is shown in the table below:

Name of branch	Congress	The Supreme Court	The President
Branch of Government	Legislature	Judiciary	Executive
Power	To make the law	To keep the law	To make decisions

In other words:

- the Congress is the legislative branch of government responsible for making the law
- the Supreme Court is the judiciary, responsible for enforcing the law
- the President, the executive branch of the government, makes decisions on the running of the country.

In reality, however, the three branches of government share many of the same functions, that is, their powers often overlap. (The Constitution was sometimes rather vague about just exactly what each Branch was entitled to do.)

For you to do

Explain what is meant by 'separation of the powers' and 'checks and balances'. Give examples to illustrate your answers.

Checks and balances

To make sure that no single branch of government becomes too powerful, a system of **checks and balances** is built in. The following shows how some of these checks and balances work.

- The President suggests most new laws but Congress must pass them.
- Congress passes the laws but the Supreme Court can reject them if they do not fit in with the rest of the Constitution.
- The President can appoint new Supreme Court judges if a vacancy occur but Congress must approve the appointment.
- The President draws up the Budget but Congress votes the money.
- The President can veto (block) a law but Congress can overturn the veto if it has a two-thirds majority.

Legislative function
The Congress
House of Representatives;
Senate
House and Senate can veto each other's bills

Congress approves presidential nominations and controls the budget. It can pass laws over the President's veto. It can impeach the President and remove him or her from office.

The President uses Congress to present Bills. The President can veto congressional legislation.

Executive function
The President
Executive office of the President; executive and cabinet departments; independent government agencies; Civil service

The Supreme Court can declare laws unconstitutional.

The Senate confirms the President's nomination. Congress can impeach judges and remove them from office.

The President nominates judges.

The Supreme Court can declare Presidential acts unconstitutional.

Judicial function
The Courts
Supreme Court; Courts of Appeal; District courts

Participation and representation

Not all of the different population groups in the USA are equally represented and some do not participate as much as others. For example, following the mid-term election in 2006, the representation of women and minorities in the 110th Congress was as follows:

Population group	% of Members of Congress	% of the Population
Women	16	51
Hispanics	5	14
Blacks	8	13

Voter turnout

Turnout at elections (the percentage of people eligible to vote who actually turn out to vote) in the USA is lower than in the UK. In the USA the average voter turnout for the last three Presidential elections is around 52% of those eligible to vote

The following figures are from the US Census Bureau for the 2004 Presidential election.

- Women turned out at a slightly higher rate (65%) than men (62%).

- Non-Hispanic white citizens voted in proportionately higher numbers (67%) than African-Americans (60%), Hispanics (47%) and Asians (44%).

- Turnout rates increased from the 2000 election among whites (by 5%) and blacks (by 3%), but held steady for Hispanics and Asians.

- Voters educated to degree level or above voted at much higher rates (80%) than those with high school degrees (56%) and those without a diploma or its equivalent (40%).

- Employed people were more likely go to the polls (66%) than the unemployed (51%).

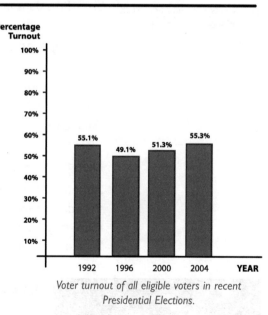

Voter turnout in presidential elections

Voter turnout of all eligible voters in recent Presidential Elections.

For you to do

- Describe the recent trend in voter turnout for Presidential elections.
- Use the information from the 2004 Presidential election turnout to create a table showing the turnout rates for different groups in the population.

REASONS FOR LOWER LEVELS OF MINORITY PARTICIPATION AND REPRESENTATION

Social reasons

Education

The more educated a person is the more likely they are to understand the issues in politics and the more likely they are to vote. Many African-Americans and Hispanics have fewer years in school and college than white people.

Discrimination

Many voters will not vote for someone from a different ethnic group. There has only ever been one non-WASP (White Anglo-Saxon Protestant) President and there has never been a non-white President of the USA; however this is about to change. The Democratic candidate for the presidential election in November 2008 was Barack Obama. Due to his election, he will be the first black President in the country's history.

Barack Obama – the first Black President of the USA

Language and culture

Some groups speak languages other than English as their first language. Many older Hispanics speak Spanish as a first language and English second. This may make politics more difficult to understand as it is mostly reported in English in the media.

Living patterns

Although African-Americans and Hispanics are concentrated in inner-city areas, they do not make up an overall majority of voters in any one state. So while there may be more minorities elected at the local level, there are very few Senators or Governors who are African-American or Hispanic.

Economic reasons

Poverty

Many poor people are simply too busy just surviving to participate in politics.

Poverty and unemployment can lead to problems of homelessness, preventing people from being able to register to vote.

Unemployment

Having a job gives people a sense of being an important part of society. Being out of work for a long time makes some people think 'society doesn't care about me so why should I care about politics?'

Political reasons

Low voter registration
US citizens must register to be allowed to vote and registration is usually lower among ethnic minorities (see figures above).

Losing faith in politics
Some African-Americans and Hispanics who voted in the past feel the government has not done much to improve their lives. Many give up voting for this reason.

Reasons why ethnic minority groups are increasingly likely to participate in politics in the USA

- There are more positive role models, e.g. Barack Obama, Condoleezza Rice.
- The black middle class is increasing: more are graduating from college, so are more likely to register to vote and therefore vote.
- The concentration of ethnic groups in particular areas of cities means that they have a better chance of getting ethnic representation.
- Voting campaigns increasingly target ethnic minorities.
- It is easier to register to vote than it used to be. See 'Motor Voter Law' on page 67.

For you to do

- In your own words describe two social, two political and two economic reasons why minorities have traditionally participated less in politics than white people.
- Now, do the same again, but this time say why minorities may be increasing their participation in politics in the USA.

HINTS & TIPS

In the exam you might be asked to organise your answer under the headings 'Social', 'Political' and 'Economic'. Some things you might include are:

- **Social (the way people live, quality of life): housing, health, education, discrimination, crime levels, family type (e.g. single parent).**
- **Political (to do with representation and participation): voter turnout, numbers of elected representatives, leaders.**
- **Economic (wealth, poverty): average wages, wage differences between groups (e.g. black and white), types of jobs, unemployment levels, poverty levels.**

INEQUALITY IN THE USA

Although the USA is a very wealthy country, there are many people from all ethnic groups, including whites, who suffer social, economic and political inequality. The 'gap' is more obvious between whites and other ethnic groups but many of the same reasons for inequality can be applied to groups such as women. Although, overall, the gap continues to narrow over time, there are still significant differences in many areas. Why does this inequality continue?

Social inequality

- **Education:** As in many other countries the standard of schools will vary greatly. Those who attend 'good' schools, perhaps in the suburbs or in the private sector, are more likely to do well than those in inner-city areas with much higher dropout rates.
- **Health:** Poorer health and less access to health care – remember, people have to pay for health care in the USA and many can't afford this or rely on the basic Medicare and Medicaid schemes.
- **Housing:** Wealthy people tend to live in the suburbs where they can afford houses that are of better quality. Others may live in the more run-down inner-city areas (ghetto areas) where housing can be very poor.

Economic inequality

- **Discrimination:** People may be unfairly treated due to factors such as race, gender and religion.
- **Wealth:** America has a very high standard of living and most Americans are in work. However, many have very poorly paid jobs and may have to rely on benefits. In the USA welfare payments are low compared to the average wage.
- **Jobs:** There are higher unemployment rates among minorities, women and people with few qualifications.

Reasons for inequality affecting minorities

- **Unemployment:** there are higher levels of unemployment among African-American and Hispanic groups.
- **Education:** there are fewer school and college qualifications among African-Americans and Hispanics.
- **Discrimination:** particularly against African-Americans and Hispanics in the work force.
- **Family structure:** there are higher numbers of single-parent families among minorities. This increases the chances of poverty.
- **Welfare cutbacks:** most recent governments in the USA have reduced welfare spending. Minorities rely more on benefits than white people.
- **Affirmative Action Programmes:** these have been cut back by the government, challenged in court or abandoned by companies fearful of being sued for discriminating against white people.
- **Lack of participation and representation:** minority turnout at elections is low, so political parties do not 'chase' the minority vote as much as the white vote. Parties have fewer policies aimed just at minorities.
- **Cost:** the cost of 'fixing' inequality would be enormous and would involve raising taxes. Politicians are reluctant to raise taxes for fear of losing elections.
- **The white flight and the circle of deprivation:** in many US major cities there are distinct areas where most of the residents are minority ethnic groups. This is known as 'de facto' segregation, i.e. it is not brought about by any rules or laws, but is the result of people separating themselves from each other by choice or because they cannot afford to live anywhere else. The following diagrams help to explain this.

  This process continued throughout the 20th century. From the 1960s onwards, many members of ethnic minorities became middle

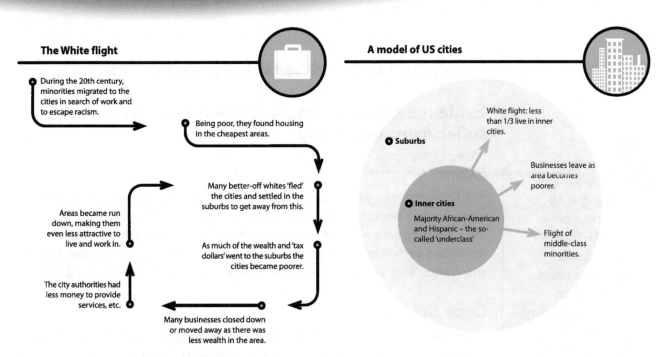

The White flight

During the 20th century, minorities migrated to the cities in search of work and to escape racism.

Being poor, they found housing in the cheapest areas.

Many better-off whites 'fled' the cities and settled in the suburbs to get away from this.

Areas became run down, making them even less attractive to live and work in.

As much of the wealth and 'tax dollars' went to the suburbs the cities became poorer.

The city authorities had less money to provide services, etc.

Many businesses closed down or moved away as there was less wealth in the area.

A model of US cities

White flight: less than 1/3 live in inner cities.

Suburbs

Businesses leave as area becomes poorer.

Inner cities
Majority African-American and Hispanic – the so-called 'underclass'

Flight of middle-class minorities.

class with good jobs and then they too 'fled' to the suburbs – the so-called 'middle class black flight'. The result is the kind of pattern we see above showing a 'Model of US cities'.

As you can see, this process produces a class of people in the inner cities sometimes referred to as an 'underclass' – people who are more likely to be out of work, living on welfare, involved in crime, etc.

The circle of deprivation

In the USA and other countries, people from poorer backgrounds often find it more difficult to succeed than those from better-off backgrounds. This diagram attempts to explain this process.

For you to do

- Explain why, historically, there have been lower levels of participation and representation among minorities in the USA.
- Why do some groups suffer from inequality in the USA?
- Imagine you are the Federal Government of the USA and you are determined to break the circle of deprivation. Describe the policies you would introduce to try to do this.

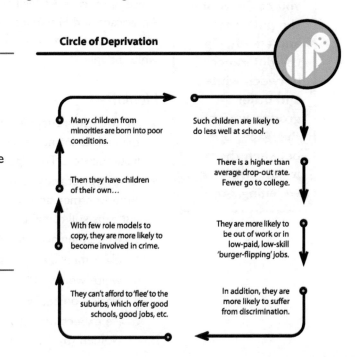

Circle of Deprivation

Many children from minorities are born into poor conditions.

Such children are likely to do less well at school.

There is a higher than average drop-out rate. Fewer go to college.

Then they have children of their own…

With few role models to copy, they are more likely to become involved in crime.

They are more likely to be out of work or in low-paid, low-skill 'burger-flipping' jobs.

They can't afford to 'flee' to the suburbs, which offer good schools, good jobs, etc.

In addition, they are more likely to suffer from discrimination.

INEQUALITY – SOME HARD FACTS

Evidence that African-Americans and Hispanics suffer from inequality

Income

In 2006, white men earned an average $20,000 more than Hispanic men, who earn less than any other other ethnic group. Asian men and women were the highest earners, with averages incomes of $50,169 and $38,613. African-Americans earned more than native Americans, but still earned less than Asians and Whites, with average incomes for men and women of $34,480 and $30,398

Crime and justice

- Murder is the leading cause of death among young African-American males aged 15–34. (The murder rate goes up as poverty increases.)
- An African-American person who kills a white person is eleven times more likely to be given the death sentence than a white person who kills an African-American person.
- Almost half the US prisoners are from minorities. There are more young African-American men in jail than attending college. (Whites make up 66% of the population.)

Employment

The unemployment rate for African-Americans is almost double the rate for white Americans. As well as being more likely to be unemployed, African-Americans and Hispanics are more concentrated in low-paid, part-time, temporary and unskilled work (sometimes called 'burger-flipping jobs') than white people.

Health

- **Infant mortality:** African-American infant deaths are 2_ times higher than white infant deaths due to poorer diet, living conditions, lack of health insurance, etc. This figure has remained the same or got worse since 1980.
- **Life expectancy:** Life expectancy is improving overall (white and African-American men and women have reached their highest ever life expectancies) but gaps still remain:
  - white men are: 75.4 years (death rate down 2.1%)
  - black men: 69.2 years (death rate down 2.5%)
  - white women: 80.5 years (death rate down 1.2%)
  - black women: 76.1 years (death rate down 2.4%)
  - life expectancy also improved for Hispanic men (by 4.2%), Hispanic women (by 1.8%), and Asian-Pacific Islander men (by 3.8%)

- **Health insurance:** In 2006, 10.5% of whites, 16% of blacks and 33.1% of Hispanics had no health insurance.

Education

Just over half of American Indian, Hispanic and African American teenagers graduate from high school compared with nearly three-quarters of Asian and White teenagers.

Only 14% of American Indian teenagers and 16% of Hispanic teenagers leave school ready to go to college, compared with 37% of white teenagers and 38% of Asian teenagers.

For you to do

- Make a list of the above factors and note whether each is a social, a political or an economic factor.

Evidence of African-American and Hispanic progress in recent years

You may be asked to describe levels of progress rather than levels of inequality so you need to have some evidence on the 'plus' side too.

Social class

There is a growing African-American middle class. Today, 47% of African-Americans are described as middle class (75% of white people are middle class).

Poverty

The overall rate in poverty for all races has declined from 20.8% in 1959 to 12.3% in 2006.

It is estimated that the proportion of the African-American population living in poverty has declined from 54.9% in 1959 to 24.3% in 2006, and for Asians, the rate has declined from 15.3% in 1987 to 10.3% in 2006.

Living patterns

Many African-Americans have moved out of the inner city to wealthier suburbs or countryside. Today, 41% live in these areas.

Participation and representation

The number of elected African-Americans and Hispanics has increased greatly since the 1960s. In the 110th Congress, there are 42 African-Americans in the House of Representatives, and one black Senator. There were 26 Hispanics in the House of Representatives and three in the Senate. Also, there were more ethnic minority members of President Bush's cabinet than in any other administration.

Minorities are now more likely to vote now due to:

- positive role models like Condoleezza Rice and Barack Obama
- improved levels of education – the more educated are more likely to vote
- voting campaigns to encourage minorities to vote
- some areas have a high percentage of minorities in them so are more likely to elect a minority candidate.

Condoleezza Rice, American Secretary of State, 2005 – present.

AFFIRMATIVE ACTION PROGRAMMES

Attempting to tackle inequality

The US Government tried to reduce inequality by bringing in measures to help ethnic groups to overcome the unfair treatment and discrimination they had been disadvantaged by in the past. These measures were called **Affirmative Action programmes** or **Positive Discrimination**.

Several schemes have been implemented in the USA to reduce the sorts of inequality shown in the statistics on the previous pages.

Quotas and targets

Businesses had to have a quota (minimum percentage) of minorities in their workforce by a certain time.

Minority admissions schemes

A number of places in universities were kept aside for minorities.

Race norming

Scores in entrance tests for universities and some jobs were adjusted up for minority candidates.

'Head Start'

Head Start was started in 1965 as part of President Johnson's 'War on Poverty'. Bright children from poor areas were given a special intensive education. This improved their schoolwork a great deal, helping them to get good jobs, or get into college and university.

Bussing

Because the majority of African-Americans and Hispanics were concentrated in inner cities, the schools there tended to be poorer. Schools in the wealthier suburbs were better off and mostly white. Some pupils were bussed to schools outside their area to try to create better mixed schools.

Housing desegregation

Low-cost public housing (council housing) was built outside the city centre to try to break down the separation of black and white.

Federal Contract Compliance

The Federal Government, through the Office of Federal Contract Compliance, will only award contracts to companies who operate equal opportunity employment policies for women and minorities.

'Motor Voter Law'

The National Voter Registration Act, introduced by President Clinton in 1995, made it easier for people to register to vote by allowing them to do it while they were obtaining a driver's licence. By 2001, 8 million people registered using this method.

Voter redistricting

Redrawing the boundaries of some constituencies so that they contain a majority of voters from minorities has increased the number of minority candidates being elected.

The arguments for and against Affirmative Action

Affirmative Action programmes have been controversial and some states have rejected them. Race norming and quotas have been abandoned. California, for example, passed Proposition 209, which said: 'The state shall not discriminate against, or grant preferential treatment to, any individual or group on the basis of race, sex, colour, ethnicity or national origin'. Since then several other states such as Michigan and Washington have either banned similar programmes or are currently thinking about doing so.

Arguments for Affirmative Action

- It tries to overcome centuries of discrimination.
- It has created a substantial African-American and Hispanic middle class, giving young minorities more positive role models.
- It helps minorities to get the rights granted in the Constitution.

Arguments against Affirmative Action

- It discriminates against whites.
- In one way, it is against the Constitution (which guarantees equal rights) because it discriminates against whites.
- It causes ill feeling if white people are 'passed' over for a job.
- Companies may take on or promote weaker candidates in order to meet a racial quota.

For you to do

- Explain the purpose of Affirmative Action.
- Construct a summary diagram of Affirmative Action Programmes.
- Do you agree or disagree with Affirmative Action? Give reasons for your answers

IMMIGRATION

FACT

- An average of more than 1.3 million immigrants (legal and illegal) settled in the USA each year during the 1990s.
- An estimated 12 million illegal immigrants live in the United States.
- The US Census Bureau projects that immigration will increase the population of the USA from 305 million in 2008 to 439 million in 2050.
- Approximately 1 million people receive permanent residency annually.

Why is the USA an attractive place for immigrants?

As you can see from the fact box above, the USA attracts millions of people each year.

Why is this the case?

- The USA has rights and freedoms that many immigrants may not have had in their former country, e.g. the right to vote, freedom of worship, free speech.
- The USA is the world's biggest capitalist country, and it is relatively easy to start a new business. This attracts business people from other countries.
- Some people enter the USA in order to join family members already living there.
- The USA has a welfare system and a system of minimum wages, which many countries do not have. For example, the Washington State minimum wage in 2008 was $8.07 compared to the average Mexican minimum wage of $4.85.

The arguments for and against continued immigration

Because of the growing percentage of minorities compared with white people (the US Census Bureau predicts that by 2042 whites will no longer comprise more than half the population), the issue of immigration to the USA has been a controversial one in recent years. Once again, you need to understand both sides of the argument.

Arguments for continued immigration

- The USA was made successful and powerful by immigrants.
- Immigrants with special skills fill jobs where there is a skills gap.
- Immigrants fill jobs that the existing population do not want.
- Immigrants bring new cultures to be enjoyed by everyone, e.g. food, music, etc.
- Many immigrants (especially in recent years from Asia) set up their own businesses, contributing to the economy by paying tax and creating more jobs.

Arguments against continued immigration

- Some people in the existing population begin to feel 'swamped' and threatened.
- It creates racial tension among some of the population.
- Many immigrants are poor and will rely on welfare, so the welfare budget increases.
- Job competition, especially at the low-paid end, is caused by immigrants working for lower wages.
- Housing competition occurs, especially in the low cost areas.

Immigration

Hundreds protest immigration raid in small-town America

POSTVILLE, Iowa — Led by 43 women with electronic tracking bracelets on their ankles, hundreds of people from around the country marched down main street here Sunday to protest against the biggest immigration raid in US history. In the raid on a meat factory, 390 mainly Guatemalan and Mexican workers were arrested by federal agents and charged with identity theft. It was the biggest raid on a workplace in US history, as part of the government's crackdown on illegal immigration, a hot issue three months ahead of the US presidential election. An estimated 12 million illegal immigrants live in the United States. It was a key issue for Democratic and Republican White House contenders Barack Obama and John McCain. Both wooed the vote of the legal Hispanic community of about 45 million people, or 15 per cent of the US population.

The arrests have torn families apart, devastated local businesses, and left the meat plant operating at only 50 percent capacity. The protest is not only directed against the anti-immigration movement, but also the meat plant itself, which over the years has left a long trail of workplace safety and environmental violations, including amputations and spilling 40,000 gallons of turkey blood into a nearby stream. Hundreds from the communities of Chicago and Minneapolis drove for hours to Postville to publicly decry the plant's owners, who are accused of abusing the workers. Although illegal, the workers and their families were an important segment of the community. School officials anticipate many empty seats when classes resume in the fall, with students' mothers and fathers now in jail.

Legalize LA campaigns for immigration reform for migrant workers

Source: adapted from Agence France-Presse, 27 July 2008

For you to do

● Explain why the USA remains such an attractive place for immigrants.
● Draw a spider diagram showing the main points concerning immigration in the USA.

KNOWLEDGE AND UNDERSTANDING

SYLLABUS AREA 4:
International relations

THE SYLLABUS AREA EXPLAINED

In this syllabus area you will be expected to show the examiner that you have a clear understanding of the following concepts:

- need
- power.

Areas you can expect to be examined on in this syllabus area are:

1 **Alliances:**
   - reasons for European countries joining and maintaining membership of organisations and alliances such as:
     - European Union
     - NATO
     - United Nations
   - reasons for military, diplomatic and economic cooperation and conflict
   - ways in which the security interests of European countries are promoted through individual and collective measures, e.g. alliances against terrorism.

2 **Politics of aid:**
   - the needs of less economically developed countries in Africa
   - reasons for other countries and the United Nations and its agencies working to meet these needs
   - ways in which these needs are met.

ALLIANCES

Countries and some of their needs

Countries have economic needs such as:

- transport
- education
- health service
- trade links.

These needs can be met through joining an organisation such as the European Union (EU).

Countries also need strong defences. A country's defence needs are often met through cooperation with other countries. This cooperation can take the form of a military **alliance** such as NATO.

Alliance: an association formed for mutual benefit, e.g. a group of countries that cooperate to benefit each other.

Military alliances

A military alliance is when a group of countries cooperate with one another, so that if one country is attacked its allies will join forces to support it. A group of countries pooling their military resources can be very powerful and may deter other countries from attacking them. For example, the UK is not powerful enough on its own so it has cooperated with other countries to form a military alliance called the North Atlantic Treaty Organisation (NATO).

NATO Secretary General Jaap de Hoop Scheffer addressing a conference

For you to do

- In your own words, jot down what this syllabus area is about. You should mention and explain the concepts as well as what you might get asked about in the exam.
- Without reading the rest of this chapter, brainstorm what you remember or know about specific alliances, e.g. NATO, the UN, the EU.
- Do the same for the politics of aid part of syllabus area 4.
- Now check what you have jotted down against the rest of this section.
- What bits do you not remember/know?
- What strategy are you going to use to help you learn these bits?
- Try learning together with a friend. This can be done in school or at home or even in the library or local cafe. Ask each other questions and devise diagrams to help you remember things.

NATO (NORTH ATLANTIC TREATY ORGANISATION)

NATO was formed at the end of the Second World War because the USA and some western European capitalist countries were worried that the USSR would try to spread communism into western Europe.

Aims of NATO

NATO now exists to safeguard the freedom and security of its member countries by political and military means. During the last 20 years, it has also played an increasingly important role in crisis management and peacekeeping such as in former Yugoslavia and Afghanistan.

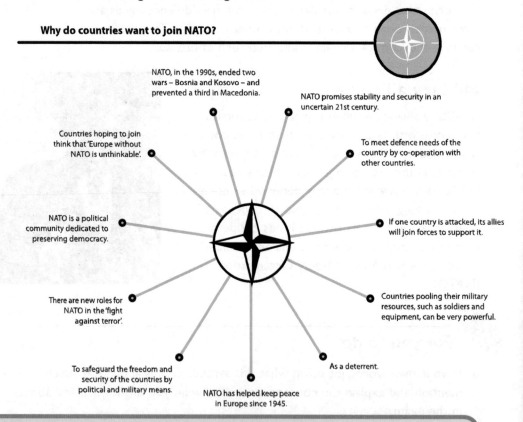

Why do countries want to join NATO?

NATO, in the 1990s, ended two wars – Bosnia and Kosovo – and prevented a third in Macedonia.

NATO promises stability and security in an uncertain 21st century.

Countries hoping to join think that 'Europe without NATO is unthinkable'.

To meet defence needs of the country by co-operation with other countries.

NATO is a political community dedicated to preserving democracy.

If one country is attacked, its allies will join forces to support it.

There are new roles for NATO in the 'fight against terror'.

Countries pooling their military resources, such as soldiers and equipment, can be very powerful.

To safeguard the freedom and security of the countries by political and military means.

As a deterrent.

NATO has helped keep peace in Europe since 1945.

Croatia and NATO

In April 2008, NATO took in two new members – Croatia and Albania. In Croatia, in January 2008, 51% of the population supported Croatian membership of NATO. Reasons for wanting to join NATO included:

- wanting to join the 'developed West'
- membership might attract investors
- membership could bring stability (Croatia was formerly part of communist Yugoslavia)
- membership of NATO could accelerate EU negotiations – Croatia wants to join the EU in 2010.

Georgia and NATO

2006: Georgian parliament voted unanimously for Georgia to be part of NATO.

2008: Georgia held a referendum on NATO membership with 77% of voters in favour of membership.

2009: Georgia hopes to gain NATO membership.

The members of NATO

- The following countries are members of NATO: USA, Canada, UK, France, Belgium, Netherlands, Luxembourg, Spain, Italy, Germany, Denmark, Iceland, Norway, Portugal, Greece, Turkey, Czech Republic, Hungary, Poland, Lithuania, Estonia, Latvia, Bulgaria, Romania, Slovakia, Slovenia, Croatia and Albania.
- Ukraine and Georgia are hoping to become members of NATO.

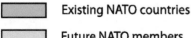 Existing NATO countries

Future NATO members

Map showing the members of the NATO alliance.

NATO IN THE 21ST CENTURY

The Prague Summit of November 2002 was a defining moment for NATO and for Europe. NATO leaders made a commitment to transform NATO to meet the new threats and security challenges of the 21st century, including terrorism and weapons of mass destruction (WMD), wherever they arise.

Decisions included:

- invite more countries to join NATO, such as Georgia and Ukraine
- improve NATO military capabilities: allies made individual commitments in key areas including, nuclear, biological and chemical (NBC) warfare protection
- create a NATO Response Force able to be deployed at short notice to wherever it is needed and sustained there for as long as necessary to achieve its objectives.

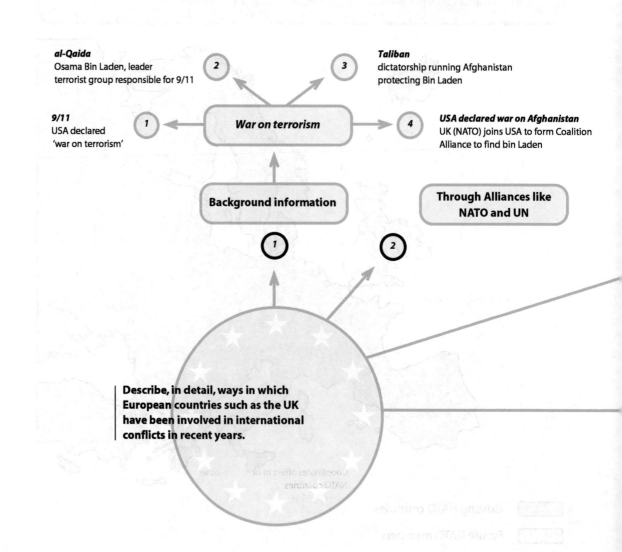

al-Qaida
Osama Bin Laden, leader terrorist group responsible for 9/11

Taliban
dictatorship running Afghanistan protecting Bin Laden

9/11
USA declared 'war on terrorism'

War on terrorism

USA declared war on Afghanistan
UK (NATO) joins USA to form Coalition Alliance to find bin Laden

Background information

Through Alliances like NATO and UN

Describe, in detail, ways in which European countries such as the UK have been involved in international conflicts in recent years.

For you to do

- What sort of *things* do countries need. See if you can get something beginning with each of these letters: THINGS.
- Explain, in detail, why some people argue there is still a need for NATO. Give at least three detailed reasons with examples.
- NATO needs to keep up with the times. The Prague Summit made various important decisions about this. Jot down two of them.
- Why is the UK involved in Afghanistan? (Clue – war on terrorism.)
- NATO is part of the coalition alliance formed by the USA as a result of the September 11 attacks. Give a detailed description of the part NATO has played in recent years in:
  - Afghanistan
  - Iraq.
- Visit the NATO website for examples of recent NATO activity.

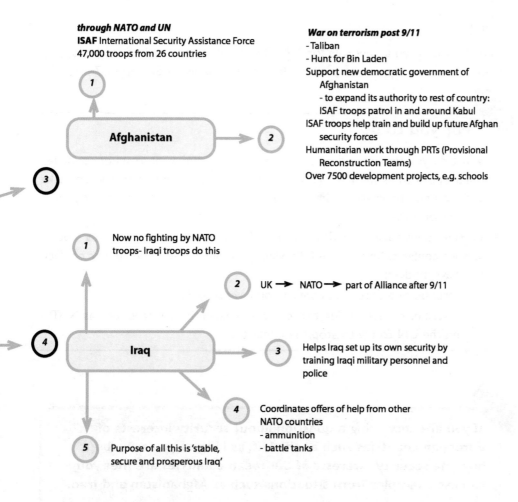

through NATO and UN
ISAF International Security Assistance Force
47,000 troops from 26 countries

1

Afghanistan → **2**

3

War on terrorism post 9/11
- Taliban
- Hunt for Bin Laden
Support new democratic government of
Afghanistan
 - to expand its authority to rest of country:
 ISAF troops patrol in and around Kabul
ISAF troops help train and build up future Afghan
 security forces
Humanitarian work through PRTs (Provisional
 Reconstruction Teams)
Over 7500 development projects, e.g. schools

1 Now no fighting by NATO
troops- Iraqi troops do this

2 UK → NATO → part of Alliance after 9/11

4 **Iraq**

3 Helps Iraq set up its own security by
training Iraqi military personnel and
police

4 Coordinates offers of help from other
NATO countries
- ammunition
- battle tanks

5 Purpose of all this is 'stable,
secure and prosperous Iraq'

THE SECURITY OF THE UK

The UK as part of the UN, the EU and NATO

The UK has involved itself in the United Nations (UN), the European Union (EU) and NATO. These are **multilateral** groups to help protect the UK's security and that of other countries, especially European countries.

The United Nations

The UK is chair of the UN Security Council Counter-Terrorism Committee (CTC). This committee helps states to analyse and meet their needs to counter terrorism.

The European Union

The UK promoted counter-terrorism measures in the EU. As a result, the EU reached agreement on common penalties for terrorist offences throughout the EU.

NATO

The UK promoted a new role for NATO in combating terrorism by deploying NATO forces in support of coalition forces in Afghanistan. See pages 74–75.

For you to do

- What do you understand by 'help protect the security interests of countries in Europe such as the UK'? This is a difficult concept to understand, so make sure you do understand it before you move on. If you are unsure ask your teacher or a friend.
- Organisations such as NATO and the UN have cooperated to try to stop various conflicts. Answer the following questions based on whatever conflict you have studied:
  - Describe one European conflict you have studied.
  - Describe, in detail, at least three actions taken by alliances such as NATO and the UN to try to stop the conflict.

WORD BANK

Multilateral: many sided; made up of many different countries.

HINTS & TIPS

If you are answering a question about security interests of European countries such as the UK, as long as you talk about how the security interests of European countries are met you can use examples from situations such as Afghanistan and Iraq.

What is being done to help protect the UK (and other countries) against terrorist attacks?

- The UK is a member of different alliances:
  - NATO, e.g. in Afghanistan to support fight against terrorism (see pages 74–75)
  - EU – promotes counter-terrorism in EU
  - member of UN Security Council Counter-Terrorism Committee

- The UK has counter-terrorism built into its foreign policy:
  - 28-day detention of terror suspects without charge
  - Counter-Terrorism Bill
    —improve public protection by strengthening arrangements for monitoring terrorists after their release from prison
    —increase penalties for terror-related offences
  - Terrorism Act 2000
    —Stop and search: seize 'articles of a kind which could be used in connection with terrorism'

- Airport security:
  - biometric passports
  - bags screened by X-ray before being put on plane
  - passengers pass through metal detectors
  - fingerprint technology – can scan and detect explosive materials
  - liquids – restrictions

This is an area that is constantly changing. Make sure you keep up to date with such security measures.

THE UNITED NATIONS (UN)

The UN is a multilateral organisation with 192 member countries. Its aim is to maintain international peace and security and to promote friendly relations between countries.

The UN Charter upholds human rights and proposes that states should work together to overcome social, economic, humanitarian and cultural challenges.

The structure of the UN

The General Assembly

The General Assembly is the main forum for debate. It is the only UN body that includes representatives from all member countries. Each member country has one vote.

The Security Council

This meets to try to attain global peace and security. Its five permanent members are China, France, Russia, the UK and the USA. It can impose economic sanctions and can authorise the use of force in conflicts. It oversees UN peacekeeping operations.

Other divisions of the UN are:

- the Economic and Social Council
- the Trusteeship Council
- the International Court of Justice
- the Secretariat.

The UN system

The UN system is made up of 14 independent agencies alongside many of the organisation's own programmes and agencies. The independent agencies include the World Bank, the International Monetary Fund (IMF) and the World Health Organisation (WHO).

UN leadership

The Secretary-General is the main spokesperson for the UN and may act as a negotiator at the highest international level. Currently Ban Ki-moon is the Secretary-General.

Some criticisms of the UN

- The war in Iraq in 2003 was launched without Security Council authorisation. This led to questions about the relevance of the UN and predictions of the collapse of the Security Council and of the entire UN system.
- Despite some successes in peacekeeping, operations in Bosnia, Rwanda and Somalia were flawed, failing to prevent massacres and genocide.
- The share-out of power in the UN, particularly in the Security Council, is hotly debated. Critics say the over-riding influence of the Council's five permanent members is unfair.

FACT

The UN does not have its own army. Troops from member countries join together to form a UN unit such as the Blue Berets – the UN Peacekeepers.

The Blue Berets.

How does the UN settle disputes?

The UN helps settle disputes by:

- peace-keeping – UN member countries send in peacekeepers to make sure peace is kept. This can range from monitoring the withdrawal of soldiers from a conflict area to supervising elections, e.g. UNAMID – UN/African Union Mission in Darfur.
- ceasefires – the UN acts as a mediator to get both sides to end the conflict.
- no-fly zones – the UN prevents aircraft from flying over an area.
- economic sanctions such as restricting the importing, exporting and manufacturing of weapons in a specific country.

For you to do

Write your own notes on ways in which the UN can help settle disputes. Make sure you have details and correct examples.

Kosovo

Kosovo became independent in June 2008 when power was transferred to the majority ethnic Albanian government after 9 years of UN rule. More than 40 countries have recognised its independence, including most EU nations.

Under a plan drawn up by the UN, an EU group called **EULEX** will operate under the auspices of **UNMIK**; EULEX aims to assist and support Kosovo authorities in the rule of law. The EU staff will consist of police officers, judges, customs officials, etc. Also, NATO troops called **K-FOR** will remain responsible for Kosovo's security and will train a new 2500-member security force in Kosovo.

EULEX: European Union Rule of Law Mission in Kosovo

UNMIK: United Nations Interim Administration Mission in Kosovo

K-FOR: Kosovo Force

ECONOMIC ALLIANCE: THE EUROPEAN UNION

The aims of the European Union (EU)

- To promote economic and social progress (help people earn enough money and be treated fairly).
- To speak for the EU on the international scene (by working as a group the EU hopes that Europe will be listened to more by other countries).
- To introduce European citizenship (anyone from a member state is a citizen of the EU).
- To develop Europe as an area of freedom, security and justice (to help Europeans live in safety, without the threat of war).
- To maintain and build on established EU law (make laws that protect people's rights in the member countries).

Joining the EU

Countries have to prove certain things in order to join the EU.

- They must show that they treat their people fairly, respect their human rights and allow them to vote in elections.
- They must show that their economies are properly run, that is, they must show that their government is sensible about the amount of money it spends and does not interfere too much in the way people do business.
- Countries may have to make changes to their laws so that they do not clash with the laws of the EU.

Countries want to join the EU mainly for economic reasons. When they join, members become part of a large and powerful economic alliance, which means that they have more countries to sell their goods to and consumers have a greater choice of goods to buy. EU citizens can live, study and work in any of the member countries. Members will cooperate over issues like human rights, terrorism and pollution.

Examples of EU economic incentives include:

- EU Structural Funds: funds the EU distributes to areas that have a poorer standard of living. Scotland gets a lot of help from these funds. Many towns and cities receive money towards building new roads to make them more accessible for businesses and tourism. These funds help to share out the wealth across the EU.
- Common Agricultural Policy (CAP): the EU helps farmers get a fair price for their products.

CONCERNS FACING THE EU

Growth

As the EU grows there will have to be changes to the structure of the Parliament and the other institutions such as the Commission. It may mean that the major players of today will lose some of their power.

The euro

Not all EU countries have taken up the euro; the UK is one of them. The 'eurozone' countries hope that using the same money will make it easier to buy and sell things to each other because they will not have to make costly and time-consuming conversions between currencies. However, decisions could be made which are good for the euro but bad for the UK. Many people in the UK want to keep the pound for sentimental and historical reasons.

Fishing

The EU wants to further limit the number of fish caught because scientists have found that the populations of many species, such as cod, are falling, and the current level of fishing is not sustainable. EU quotas have been established but fishermen argue that the new quotas will put many of them out of work, as well as many others who rely on the fishing industry for employment.

The enlarged 27-nation European Union in 2008.

For you to do

- Create a mnemonic to help you remember what sorts of economic needs a country might have. Try using the word ECONOMIC.
- Give, in detail, three reasons why countries want to join the EU.
- Jot down three ways that becoming an EU member would help a country meet its economic needs. Have two columns, 'The economic need' and 'How being an EU member helps meet that need'.
- Make up a spider diagram of at least three problems facing the EU.

Internet research

- Find out at least three facts about fishing quotas in the EU.
- Why is this a big issue in the EU?

Joined in 1957
1) Belgium
2) France
3) Netherlands
4) Germany
5) Italy
6) Luxembourg

Joined in 1973
7) Denmark
8) Ireland
9) UK

Joined in 1981
10) Greece

Joined in 1981
11) Portugal
12) Spain

Joined in 1995
13) Austria
14) Finland
15) Sweden

Joined in 2004
16) Czech Republic
17) Cyprus
18) Hungary
19) Estonia
20) Latvia
21) Lithuania
22) Malta
23) Poland
24) Slovakia
25) Slovenia

Joined in 2007
26) Bulgaria
27) Romania

POLITICS OF AID

This section of syllabus area 4 looks at the needs of less economically developed countries in Africa and how these needs may be met. The concepts involved in this section are need and power.

Problems, causes and needs

PROBLEM	CAUSES	NEED
Not enough food	Too many people; not enough fertile land; drought; land used for cash crops	Improve agriculture; reduce birth rate
Poor health and health care; AIDS; high death rate	Not enough money invested in health by the government of the country; too few doctors, hospitals, etc.; people cannot get to services	Improve health care; educate the people; government to spend money
Poor education; illiteracy is high especially among girls; affects economy of country	Not enough money invested in education by government; low status of females in the country; money directed on things such as war	Improve education standards; improve status of women
Debt; dependence on cash crops	Less economically developed countries often borrow large amounts of money from rich countries to help set up businesses, cannot afford to repay loans so always in debt	Restructure the economy; start growing crops to eat; rich countries to 'drop the debt'
Wars and civil wars; undemocratic government	Civil war due to different factions disputing things like land; religious conflict; dictator running country; resources can be destroyed; refugees	Have democratic government; money focused on education, health, etc.; rich countries to stop selling arms

HINTS & TIPS

The second part of syllabus area 4 is all about politics of aid.

This part looks only at *less economically developed countries* in Africa. Africa is a continent made up of a number of separate countries. Do not use examples from South Africa in your answers to questions in this part.

Aid to less economically developed countries

Rich or **more economically developed countries** can give aid to less economically developed countries.

More economically developed countries: countries that are relatively wealthy and have good infrastructure in place such as good education, health care and industry.

- Bilateral aid goes straight from one country to another (bi=two; lateral=sided). Some bilateral aid is tied, i.e. it has to be spent in a particular way, often back in the donor country. It is often called boomerang aid as it also benefits the country it came from.
- Multilateral aid is given by groups of countries or organisations such as the UN or the EU.
- Voluntary aid comes from charities or non-governmental organisations (NGOs) such as Oxfam, World Vision or the Red Cross.

Why do countries like UK give aid?

Aid from the UK is given through the Department for International Development (DFID). Donor countries such as the UK will take many factors into account before giving aid to less economically developed countries in Africa.

Social factors

- Education levels within the recipient country: how many people can read or write?
- Unemployment levels in donor and recipient countries: will aid reduce unemployment or increase it in the donor country?
- Birth and death rates and other health factors: how bad are they?

Economic factors

- Can the donor country afford to give aid?
- Is any of the aid 'tied aid'?
- Will the donor country benefit?
- Will aid help the recipient country's economy?
- Does the recipient country have important natural resources such as oil?

Political factors

- Is the recipient country a friend or foe?
- Is the recipient country run by a democratic government?
- Is its human rights record good or bad?

Millennium Development Goals (MDGs)

- MDGs are eight goals to be achieved by 2015 that are set up to meet the world's main development challenges (problems).
- They have been adopted by 189 nations (September 2000).
- The eight goals are:
  - eradicate extreme poverty and hunger
  - achieve universal primary education
  - promote gender equality
  - reduce child mortality
  - improve maternal health
  - combat HIV/AIDS, malaria and other diseases
  - ensure environmental sustainability
  - develop a Global Partnership for Development.

BILATERAL AID FOR KENYA

The following case study will provide good examples for you to use to illustrate answers to questions relating to the politics of aid.

Kenya: development indicators (2008)

Development indicators show the level of development in a country. They can be social, economic or political.

Population: 34.5 million

Social indicators

1 **Health:**
   - Average life expectancy: 45 years (UK: 78 years)
   - Children dying before age 5: 115 per 1,000 live births (UK: 6 per 1,000 live births)
   - Women dying in childbirth: 414 per 100,000 live births (UK: 9 per 100,000 live births)
   - 5.1% of the adult population lives with HIV/AIDS (about 1.1 million people). In the UK the number is around 60,000 (0.1%).

2 **Education:**
   - Percentage of children receiving primary school education: 86%.

Economic indicators

- Average per capita income: US$580 (UK:£19600 = US$37,600)
- Percentage of people not meeting daily food needs: 46% are living below food poverty line.

Political indicators

- Grand Coalition Government formed in February 2008 after a disputed general election led to widespread violence and ethnic division.
- Corruption is a significant problem in Kenya.

Source: Department for International Development

UK aid to Kenya (through DFID)

Governance: the method, processes and policies of management (government) of a country.

DFID's primary aim in Kenya is to reduce poverty in line with the MDGs. DFID has focused its spending on three main sectors:

- education
- health and HIV/AIDS
- **governance**.

In the financial year 2007/08 DFID provided £50 million in assistance.

Health

12.8 million new insecticide treated bednets (ITNs) have contributed to a 44% reduction in child mortality.

DFID has provided £45 million towards the fight against HIV and AIDS.

DFID aims to sell 172 million condoms from 2003 to 2009. This will avert an estimated 85,000 cases of HIV.

Education

DFID has committed £55 million to the education sector (2005 2010). This is providing teaching and learning materials, improving teachers' skills and 4,500 schools are getting new primary school classrooms and better water and sanitation facilities.

Progress in achieving the Millennium Development Goals:

- Kenya is making strong progress on primary education. 86% of children are enrolled in primary schools (compared to 62% in 1992) and gender equality in primary school is now at 98%.
- HIV/AIDS prevalence has fallen from more than 11% in 2003 to 5.1% in 2008.

For you to do

- You need to know about the needs of countries in Africa and how these needs are met. Make up a diagram to show four needs.
  - Give examples from countries in Africa.
  - Say why meeting that need is a problem in that country.
  - Say what needs to be done to help solve that need.
- Countries in need get aid. Describe the three main types of aid and for each type of aid give one good thing and one bad thing about that type of aid.
- The UK gives its aid through a government organisation called DFID. What are the aims of DFID?
- If you were employed by DFID and had to decide if a country in Africa was to get aid from DFID, what sorts of questions would you ask (social, economic and political)?
- What evidence is there that Kenya is a less economically developed country? Use the development indicators and think back to the types of questions you would ask in the previous question.
- Give, in detail, three examples of aid. You may want to search out more information from the Internet. Use the DFID website.

HINTS & TIPS

This book uses Kenya as an example of a less economically developed country in Africa that receives aid. You will have looked at other countries. In your answers in the exam you can use whatever country in Africa (except South Africa) you know about.

MULTILATERAL AID FOR KENYA

Multilateral aid

The following case studies will provide you with examples to use in the exam when answering questions on multilateral aid.

World Health Organisation (WHO)

Free health services to families: June 2008: two weeks of countrywide mobilisation for increased use of routine child survival services. The initiative, named Malezi Bora (Swahili for 'Good Nurturing'), was adopted by the Kenyan government, in partnership with the World Health Organisation, to address poor child survival indicators in Kenya.

Source: adapted from Unicef website

UNICEF: HIV/AIDS

Pepo La Tumaini Jangwani (Wind of Hope in the Desert) is a community-based HIV/AIDS support group providing medical care, education, food and a referral service to the local hospital where UNICEF is supporting ways of preventing mother-to-child transmission of the virus. UNICEF provides nutritional support through the group for hundreds of households affected by HIV/AIDS. In these homes, food consumption can drop by more than 40%, putting children at risk of malnutrition. Adequate nourishment can delay the onset of AIDS and prevent some of the illnesses associated with the disease.

Source: adapted from Unite for Children website

Food and Agricultural Organisation (FAO)

FAO supports Kenyan Government efforts to restore the agricultural production and self-reliance of rural families most affected by post-election violence (December 2007) and the projected drought.

FAO's proposed activities include:

- assisting internally displaced persons (IDPs) to resettle and resume agricultural activities
- maximising food production through the provision of seeds, tools, fertilisers and veterinary supplies
- rehabilitation of fields, pastures and key infrastructure.

Source: adapted from FAO and emergencies web page

For you to do

- Remember that the UN is an example of a multilateral organisation. What does this mean?
- The UN is made up of a number of specialised agencies, some of which are crucial to giving aid to countries. List three of these specialised agencies.
- In what ways do UN specialised agencies help meet the needs of people in Kenya?
- On a large piece of paper do the following:
  - draw a quick map of Africa and mark on Kenya
  - jot down three actions that UN agencies have taken recently in Kenya.

  Learn the information before you write it down. Put the poster up somewhere prominent.

TeleFood projects

TeleFood is part of the Food and Agricultural Organisation (FAO). The money is mostly raised through television concerts. Bands will put on a free concert that will be televised and people will pledge money.

TeleFood projects are designed to give families and communities the tools necessary to increase the quantity and variety of food they produce. Every project is regularly monitored and audited. Today, the results of TeleFood can be seen in over 1000 projects in more than 100 countries.

TeleFood projects range from crop production to fish and animal production. Crop production projects provide essential vitamins and minerals that are often lacking in diets. They also generate income, since excess crops can be sold in local markets. Animal and fish production projects provide valuable sources of protein and provide nourishment between crop harvests.

Source: fao.org

For you to do

The Food and Agricultural Organisation (FAO) is one of the agencies of the UN. Part of its work is a project called TeleFood. Make your own notes about TeleFood and what it does to meet the needs of countries in Africa. Try listing three needs and say how each need is met by a TeleFood project. You may want to get more information on the TeleFood website.

Internet research

Find out more about UNAIDS. This can be used as a good example in your answers.

AIDS is a huge problem in many less economically developed countries in Africa. UNAIDS helps meet the needs of these countries. Look up the website and choose an example that you can use in your exam.

ROLE OF VOLUNTARY ORGANISATIONS IN HELPING DEVELOPING COUNTRIES IN AFRICA

Voluntary organisations (charities and NGOs) have a vital role in helping developing countries in Africa to meet the needs of their populations. These case studies give examples of the kind of work done to help combat poverty and disease.

FARM-Africa: Kenya

Dairy goat and capacity building project

This project aims to reduce poverty for the small-scale farmers by increasing the productivity of dairy goats and providing access to animal healthcare. Goats are offered only to 'the poorest of the poor', but in countries where there are so many poor it is difficult to work out who these people are. Farm-Africa's method, after drawing up a set of poverty indicators – How often do they eat? How overcrowded is their house? Do they have any land? – is to coordinate villagers so they can do it themselves. The aim of the project it to cross Toggenburgs with local goats, producing animals with resilience to local diseases but a much higher milk production. Breeders are chosen because they have many children and are thus grateful for the extra milk which reduces the incidence of diseases such as kwashiorkor.

Source: The Guardian, November 8 2005

FARM Africa
Making a lasting difference to Africa's families

For you to do

Countries in Africa get help from voluntary organisations. Make your own notes on the following:

- Why is FARM-Africa involved in Kenya? (What needs is it trying to meet?)
- What help does FARM-Africa give Kenya?
- How successful do you think this help is? Give reasons for your answer.

For you to do

Countries in Africa get help from voluntary organisations. Make your own notes on the following:

- Why is VETAID involved in Kenya? (What needs is it trying to meet?)
- What help has VETAID given to Kenya?
- How successful do you think this help is? Give reasons for your answer.

VETAID: Kenya

VETAID carried out a mass vaccination campaign in Kenya in July 2008.

The campaign focused on livestock belonging to people living in makeshift camps for internally displaced people (IDPs). These people were forced to flee their homes during the post-election violence at the beginning of 2008.

Nearly 16,000 animals in Kenya's Rift Valley were vaccinated against rabies and foot and mouth disease. The animals were vaccinated as a result of a VETAID assessment. This was one of the areas most affected by the violence and the impact upon livestock numbers and animal health was huge.

Some IDPs were still living with their animals in the camps which lacked essential care and shelter as well as space and grazing land. The owners were unable to access animal feeds because of the disrupted supply, due to road blocks and fuel shortages, and have to share some human food with the animals.

Source: Vetaid.org

ActionAid: Kenya

Thakara women water users association

act:onaid

Women traditionally played a minimal role in development activities in Thakara, partly because they were not allowed to sit in meetings with men. Women were expected to do most of the household chores and would walk up to 15km a day to collect water.

Consultation with the Thakara community revealed that access to clean water was their main problem and ActionAid Kenya identified a local river as a potential source of piped water. After several discussions it was agreed to put women in charge of the project to reflect their traditional role. Women were trained in management techniques, protection of the water supply, maintenance techniques and record keeping. This improved their confidence, self-esteem and power in the community. Eleven separate kiosk management committees were set up and 14,000 households now have easy access to clean water. Profits from the kiosks have been used to run education courses.

Source: ActionAid.org.uk

For you to do

Countries in Africa get help from voluntary organisations. Make your own notes on the following:

- Why is ActionAid involved in Kenya? (What needs is it trying to meet?)
- What help does ActionAid give Kenya?
- How successful do you think this help is? Give reasons for your answer.

Enquiry Skills (ES) questions make up 60% of the paper.

There are two types of Enquiry Skills questions:

- **source-based questions** (use only the sources to answer the question)
- **investigating-type questions** (look out for the logo shown here)

SOURCE-BASED QUESTIONS

Using the sources

To answer source-based enquiry skills questions you must only use the information given in the sources.

Source-based questions require lots of practice but you do not need to bring any of your own knowledge. This is important because if you use facts that you do not find in the sources you will get no extra marks and you will simply waste precious time needed to examine the sources.

There are three types of source-based questions:

- 'exaggeration' questions (in the General Paper); 'selective in use of facts' questions (in the Credit Paper).
- 'conclusion' questions
- express support of a given point of view / arguments for and against.

General and Credit questions are different. Look out for hints at each level. Credit level hints will be highlighted with this symbol.

'BUS' the questions

Read each question you come across in the exam carefully. Break it down so you know exactly what you have to do; highlight the important parts by 'bussing' the question as follows:

B = BOX (put a box around the type of question it is, e.g. exaggeration)

U = UNDERLINE (underline exactly what you have to do, e.g. 'give two reasons why ...')

S = SOURCES (circle the sources you have to use).

EXAGGERATION QUESTIONS (GENERAL PAPER)

Study Sources 1 and 2 below, then answer the question which follows.

Answering the question

This question is one where you have to detect exaggeration and give reasons to support your choice.

This is a General question and is worth 4 marks.

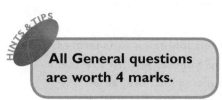

All General questions are worth 4 marks.

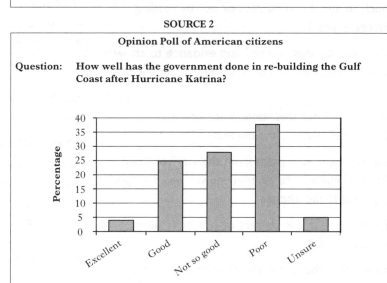

QUESTION 3 (A) (CONTINUED)

(d)   Study Sources 1 and 2 below, then answer the question which follows.

SOURCE 1

Hurricane Katrina hit the Gulf Coast of the United States on 29 August 2005, destroying towns in the states of Mississippi and Louisiana. It made one million people homeless, and killed almost 1,800 others. Americans were upset at the size of the disaster and how poorly prepared all levels of government were to deal with the problem. The President agreed that the government had been slow to respond. He promised "one of the largest re-building efforts the world has ever seen" to repair the damage.

SOURCE 2

Opinion Poll of American citizens

Question: **How well has the government done in re-building the Gulf Coast after Hurricane Katrina?**

Hurricane Katrina caused a great deal of damage to the Gulf Coast area. However, the government was well equipped to respond to the disaster. President Bush has promised to re-build these states. The majority of people agree that the government is doing a good re-building job.

View of Reed Johnson

Using **only** Source 1 and Source 2 above, write down **two** statements made by Reed Johnson which are **exaggerated**.

Using the information in the Sources, give **one** reason why **each** of the statements you have chosen is **exaggerated**.

(Enquiry Skills, **4** marks)

'BUS' the question

Using **only** Source 1 and Source 2 above, write down **two** statements made by Reed Johnson which are **exaggerated**.

Using the information in the Sources, give **one** reason why **each** of the statements you have chosen is **exaggerated**.

You have to copy out (write down) two statements from the view of Reed Johnson that are exaggerated (not correct) based on the evidence in sources 1 and 2.

Read the view of Reed Johnson carefully. There are four statements. Two are exaggerated (not correct) and two are correct.

Read the first sentence from the view of Reed Johnson: *Hurricane Katrina caused a great deal of damage to the Gulf Coast area.*

Check to see if it is correct or not by reading sources 1 and 2.

When you do this you will find evidence to show that this statement is correct. The evidence is in source 1.

Do not copy out this statement since it is not exaggerated (that is, it is correct).

Read the next statement from the view of Reed Johnson: *However, the government was well equipped to respond to the disaster.*

Check to see if it is correct or not by reading sources 1 and 2.

You will find there is evidence in source 1 to show that this statement is exaggerated//incorrect. Source 1 says '*Americans were upset at the size of the disaster and how poorly prepared all levels of government were to deal with the problem.*'

Now you can start to write out the answer to the question:

This statement by Reed Johnson is exaggerated: 'However, the government was well equipped to respond to the disaster.' The reason it is exaggerated is because in source 1 it says that 'Americans were upset at the size of the disaster and how poorly prepared all levels of government were to deal with the problem.' The President himself also recognised the government's slow response.

Now go back and read the third statement in the view: *President Bush has promised to re-build these states.* Check the sources to see if there is evidence to show that this statement is exaggerated. You will find that, in source 1, there is evidence to show the statement is correct. So do not copy it out.

Therefore the last/fourth statement in the view must be exaggerated/incorrect. Check the sources to see if there is evidence to show it is exaggerated. There is evidence in source 2.

So you can now continue your answer by writing out the fourth statement by Reed Johnson:

This statement by Reed Johnson is exaggerated: 'The majority of people agree that the President is doing a good re-building job.' The reason it is exaggerated is because source 2 says that only about 30% of American citizens say that the government has done a good job in re-building the Gulf Coast after the hurricane. This is not a majority and so the statement is exaggerated.

So your final answer will look like this:

This statement by Reed Johnson is exaggerated: 'However, the government was well equipped to respond to the disaster.' The reason it is exaggerated is because in source 1 it says that 'Americans were upset at the size of the disaster and how poorly prepared all levels of government were to deal with the problem.' The President himself also recognised the government's slow response.

This statement by Reed Johnson is exaggerated: 'The majority of people agree that the President is doing a good re-building job.' The reason it is exaggerated is because source 2 says that only about 30% of American citizens say that the government has done a good job in re-building the Gulf Coast after the hurricane. This is not a majority and so the statement is exaggerated.

Marking

The sample answer above gets full 4 marks:

- it uses both sources
- the two exaggerated (incorrect) statements are copied out (1 mark each)
- for each exaggerated statement, one correct reason is identified from the sources (1 mark each).

For you to do

Using the SQA Past Papers, find some more exaggeration questions at General level. Answer them and check your answer with the answer section in the Past Papers. Ask your teacher to check them over.

SELECTIVE IN THE USE OF FACTS (CREDIT PAPER)

QUESTION 3 (A) (CONTINUED)

(c) Study the information in Sources 1, 2 and 3 below and on the next page, then answer the question which follows.

SOURCE 1

The Rockford Record

Your local voice, free to all 10 000 homes in Rockford City (23 May 2008)

New Housing Project Causes Local Anger

A recent public meeting in Rockford City Hall was attended by 500 local people. They were told about plans for a new gated community of 700 houses called "Red Pines". It is to be built by the Allan Building Company.

The gated community of Red Pines would be a walled housing development to which public access would be restricted. It would be guarded using CCTV and security personnel. The complex would have its own supermarkets, restaurants and bars.

The people at the meeting showed mixed feelings, for and against the possible development.

In 2004, gated communities housed 16 million Americans, about 6% of all households. Homeowners in gated communities live in upmarket and mostly white developments. Affluent black American homeowners are less likely than white people to live in gated communities.

The Red Pines Area Now

At the moment Red Pines is a beautiful wooded area. It is used by Rockford residents for walking and exercise. There is a jogging track, 3 football pitches and a rowing club on the river. Unfortunately, it floods occasionally as it is near to the river.

Doctor Joan Quincy said, "It is well known that Rockford residents are not very good at taking exercise. Health statistics show that compared to the rest of the USA we need to take more exercise. We need

Health and Exercise Statistics	Rockford	USA
Overweight	48%	35%
Bicycle riding	6%	16%
Exercise walking	16%	32%
Running/Jogging	4%	10%

the Red Pines area to keep our people healthy. We want to encourage more people to exercise in this area. Building houses would be a disaster for our community."

The building of Red Pines would also cause a great deal of disturbance in and around the town. There might be a few short-term benefits for the local community but long-term, there will be no real gain for the town as those living in Red Pines are unlikely to be spending much money in the shops in Rockford. They will get in their cars and drive to the city which is only 15 miles away.

Doctor Quincy is also Chairperson of the Rockford Residents' Association.

QUESTION 3 (A) (c) (CONTINUED)

SOURCE 2

What the people want

The Rockford Record decided to find out the views of local people about the "Red Pines" development. We conducted an opinion poll and received 8900 replies from 10 000 homes and feel that this survey shows the real views of the people.

The Questions: How Important	Unimportant	Not very important	Important	Very important
is it that Rockford stays a racially mixed town?	20%	15%	25%	40%
a problem is jobs to the people of Rockford?	15%	25%	20%	40%
is the Red Pines area for exercise?	20%	10%	45%	25%

Ethnic origin of Rockford's Residents

Other 8%
White 32%
Hispanic 29%
Black 31%

SOURCE 3

Leaflet from Allan Building Company

I am Chairman of the Allan Building Company and I was born in Rockford. I have stayed here all my life and want to do the best for Rockford. There is great demand for this type of housing from middle and upper income groups who would not live in Rockford because of their fear of rising crime there. We already have 500 new families from outwith Rockford, wanting to move into Red Pines whenever it is built. They are a mixture of young and old with an ethnic mix of 50% White, 25% Hispanic, 24% Black and 1% other groups.

Impact on Rockford

SHORT-TERM IMPACT	LONG-TERM IMPACT
• Skilled workers employed in the building of Red Pines. • Unskilled workers also needed. • Workers on-site spend money in local shops. • Building supply companies will increase trade.	• Unskilled jobs will be available, eg cleaners. • Jobs will be available in the new shops and restaurants. • Shops in Rockford will gain extra business from the new residents close-by. • Local shops have the opportunity to become suppliers to the new restaurants and bars which will open. • Flood prevention measures will stop flooding.

The Red Pines gated development will cause many problems for our health and change the ethnic mix of Rockford. It will bring few benefits to the people of Rockford.

View of Findlay Smith, Editor, The Rockford Record

Using **only** the information in Sources 1, 2 and 3, explain, **in detail**, **the extent to which** Findlay Smith could be accused of being **selective in the use of facts**.

(Enquiry Skills, **8** marks)

Answering the question

'BUS' the question

Credit questions can be worth 4, 6, 8 or 10 marks.

> Using **only** the information in Sources 1, 2 and 3, explain, in detail, the extent to which Findlay Smith could be accused of being **selective in the use of facts**.

Here you have to work out how much is true and how much is not true in what the person is saying and make a judgement about how selective the person is being (the extent to which he is being selective in his use of facts).

It is important to understand how marks are allocated in this type of question.

- Up to 2 marks are given for an example of selectivity (or not).
- For full marks (this question is generally worth 8 marks), all sources must be used.
- Answers that don't make a direct link between the view and the sources will generally get a maximum of 4 marks.
- The extent/degree of selectivity is worth up to 2 marks. If no extent is specified then a maximum of 6 marks can be given.

This may sound complicated, but it isn't really. Basically, you need to give at least three examples of selectivity (or not), make direct links with all the sources and say to what extent the person can be accused of being selective.

So, read the question on Rockford carefully. In particular, read carefully the view of Findlay Smith. He says the following three things – remember you are looking for at least three examples of selectivity (or not):

- the Red Pines gated development will cause many problems for our health
- the Red Pines gated development will change the ethnic mix of Rockford
- it will bring few benefits to the people of Rockford.

You must now take each of these statements separately and give evidence from the sources to show to what extent that statement is true.

There is a lot to read in the three sources so you need to develop a strategy to cope with the amount of information. One strategy is to underline/mark/highlight the relevant information for each statement but one at a time.

For example, this is the first statement to be examined:

The Red Pines gated development will cause many problems for our health.

Write this statement down. Then look over all the sources to see if there is evidence to say that this statement is true or not. You could underline the information you think is useful. For example:

Source 1

Red Pines wooded area, at the moment, is used for walking and exercise: it has a jogging track, three football pitches and a rowing club on the river.

Dr Joan Quincy thinks that Rockford residents need more exercise.

The health statistics show that Rockford residents are more overweight than the rest of the USA (48% compared with 35%). They also take less exercise than Americans as a whole (4% run/jog compared with 10%).

Source 2

The opinion poll shows that 70% of Rockford residents think that the Red Pines area is very important/important for exercise.

So, overall, Findlay Smith is correct (not selective at all) when he says that the Red Pines gated development will cause many problems for the health of the people in Rockford as it will reduce their opportunities to exercise.

This is one way to approach answering a selective in the use of facts question. You would need to follow the above steps to cover all three of Findlay Smith's statements.

Ensure all three sources are used and that an overall comment is reached regarding the extent of selectivity. For the example here, you should find the following a suitable conclusion to your answer:

Overall extent of selectivity of Findlay Smith: Findlay Smith is correct/ not selective at all in the first two statements and wrong in the third. So, in conclusion, he is slightly selective in his use of facts.

Some words you might want to use regarding the extent of selectivity are:

- entirely selective
- mostly selective
- slightly selective
- not selective at all.

There are many more for you to think up!

For you to do

Using the SQA Past Papers, find some more similar selective in the use of facts questions at Credit level. Answer these and check your answer with the answer section in the Past Papers. Ask your teacher to check them over.

CONCLUSION QUESTIONS (GENERAL PAPER)

This type of question requires you to compare and contrast information in a number of different sources and then come to some **conclusions**.

Conclusion: a decision or a judgement that you reach by reasoning.

To reach your conclusion you have to work out what the points of the sources are, and use the information to back up a number of decisions/conclusions. A conclusion must be backed up with evidence; it is not just a summary of the main points. If you simply summarise the main points you will not get good marks.

QUESTION 4 (CONTINUED)

(b) Study the information below, then answer the question which follows.

Data for selected NATO countries

Country	1990		2005	
	Numbers in Armed Forces ('000s)	Defence spending per person ($)	Numbers in Armed Forces ('000s)	Defence spending per person ($)
Greece	201	500	209	610
UK	308	770	216	530
USA	2,181	1,400	1,492	925
Turkey	769	110	816	115

Write down **two** conclusions about Armed Forces and Defence spending.

You should write **one** conclusion **with evidence** about **each** of the following.

• The country with the biggest change in the numbers in its armed forces.

• What happens to the numbers in the armed forces as defence spending rises.

You **must** only use the information above.

(Enquiry Skills, **4** marks)

[Turn over

Answering the question

'BUS' the question

> Write down **two** conclusions about Armed Forces and Defence spending.
> You should write **one** conclusion **with evidence** about **each** of the following.
> - The country with the biggest change in the numbers in its armed forces.
> - What happens to the numbers in the armed forces as defence spending rises.
>
> You **must** only use the information above.

Read the actual question **carefully** ... not the **source** but the 'Write down ...' section.

This question is very specific in telling you what you have to do. You have to write down two conclusions about Armed Forces and Defence spending. It then tells you in detail what your conclusions should be about – the country with the biggest change in the numbers in its armed forces, and what happens to numbers in the armed forces as defence spending rises.

Since it is an Enquiry Skills question, all the answers can be found in the sources.

Marking

Up to 2 marks can be given for each conclusion, depending on the quality of the evidence.

For this question, the following sample answer would be awarded full 4 marks:

My first conclusion is that the country with the biggest change in the number of its armed forces is the USA.

The evidence for this is that its numbers fell by less than any of the other selected NATO countries. For example, USA numbers fell by 689,000 whereas the UK fell by only 92,000.

My second conclusion is that as defence spending rises so does the number of a country's armed forces.

The evidence for this is that in Greece, the defence spending went up from $500 per person to $610 per person and at the same time the number in its armed forces rose from 201,000 to 209,000. Turkey follows a similar pattern.

For you to do

Using the SQA Past Papers, find some more conclusion questions at General level. Answer these and check your answer against the answer section in the Past Papers. Ask your teacher to check them over.

CONCLUSION QUESTIONS (CREDIT PAPER)

C

QUESTION 4 (CONTINUED)

(*c*)   Study the information in Sources 1, 2 and 3 below and on the next page, then answer the question which follows.

SOURCE 1
Millennium Development Goals

The Millennium Development Goals were agreed by 189 countries in New York in 2000.

Selected Millennium Development Goals

1:    **Reduce child mortality**

2:    **Achieve primary education for all**

3:    **Remove extreme poverty and hunger**

4:    **Combat diseases**

These goals represented a commitment by rich and poor nations to expand social and economic progress in all regions of the world, as well as creating a global partnership for reducing levels of poverty and suffering in less developed countries by 2015.

Many are now questioning the commitment of the More Developed Countries to making these goals a reality as few MDCs give the UN recommended 0·7% of Gross National Income (GNI).

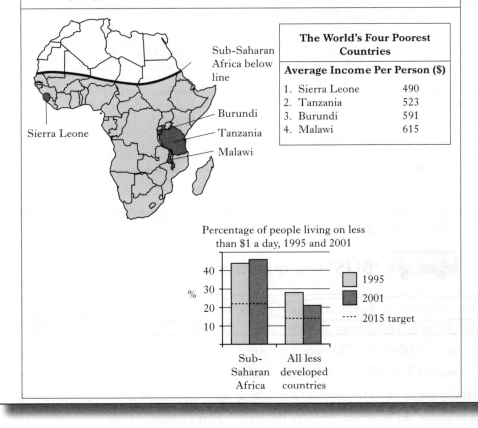

Sub-Saharan Africa below line

Sierra Leone

Burundi

Tanzania

Malawi

The World's Four Poorest Countries	
Average Income Per Person ($)	
1. Sierra Leone	490
2. Tanzania	523
3. Burundi	591
4. Malawi	615

Percentage of people living on less than $1 a day, 1995 and 2001

1995
2001
---- 2015 target

Sub-Saharan Africa

All less developed countries

QUESTION 4 (c) (CONTINUED)

SOURCE 2: Aid given by selected Donor Countries

Selected Donor Countries	Aid Given			Largest recipients ($ millions)
	2004 $ billions (% of GNI)	2010 (prediction) $ billions (% of GNI)	% increase	
UK	7·88 (0·36)	14·60 (0·59)	85	1. India ($419) 2. Bangladesh ($267) 3. Tanzania ($265)
USA	19·7 (0·17)	24·00 (0·18)	22	1. Iraq ($2286) 2. Congo ($804) 3. Egypt ($767)
Portugal	1·03 (0·63)	0·93 (0·51)	−10	1. Angola ($367) 2. Cape Verde ($39) 3. Timor ($34)
Italy	2·46 (0·15)	9·26 (0·51)	276	1. Dem. Rep. Congo ($235) 2. China ($52) 3. Tunisia ($41)

SOURCE 3

Four Poorest African Countries – Progress on selected Millennium Development Goals								
	Sierra Leone		Tanzania		Burundi		Malawi	
Selected Indicators \ Year	1996	2006	1996	2006	1996	2006	1996	2006
% of population undernourished	44	50	50	44	63	67	50	34
Child Mortality (per 1000 births)	293	283	159	126	190	190	216	175
% 1 year olds vaccinated against measles	37	64	49	91	80	75	90	80
% Primary school enrolment	43	73	94	95	43	57	48	98

Using **only** the information above and opposite, you must **make** and **justify** conclusions about progress towards the Millennium Development Goals using the **four** headings below.

- Progress towards Millennium Development Goal 1
- Progress towards **all** of Millennium Development Goal 3
- The commitment of More Developed Countries to meeting the UN aid recommendation
- The commitment of Donor Countries to the world's **four poorest** nations

(Enquiry Skills, **8** marks)

Answering the question

'BUS' the question

Using **only** the information above [and opposite], you must **make** and **justify** conclusions about progress towards the Millennium Development Goals using the **four** headings below.

- Progress towards Millennium Development Goal 1
- Progress towards **all** of Millennium Development Goal 3
- The commitment of More Developed Countries to meeting the UN aid recommendation
- The commitment of Donor Countries to the world's **four poorest** nations

It is useful in any source-based question to work out what the sources are all about. Here is an example of what you might work out using the question on the Millennium Development Goals.

Source 1 is in two parts:

- part 1 tells us what some of the MDGs are and why they were set up. The last sentence seems important: 'Many are now questioning ...'
- part 2 has (i) a map showing sub-Saharan Africa with a table showing that four of the world's poorest countries are in sub-Saharan Africa, and (ii) and a bar graph comparing the percentage of people living on less than $1/day in sub-Saharan Africa with all less developed countries.

Source 2

- table showing aid given by selected donor countries
- also shows largest recipients of aid.

Source 3

- table showing progress made by four poorest African countries from 1996 to 2006 on some of the MDGs.

Although this question looks complex, it isn't really, as long as you approach your answer logically. When you read the question it tells you to make and justify conclusions about **progress towards the MDGs.**

The question then proceeds to give you the headings that you have to draw conclusions about. There are four headings:

- Progress towards Millennium Development Goal 1
- Progress towards all of Millennium Development Goal 3
- The commitment of More Developed Countries to meeting the UN aid recommendation
- The commitment of Donor Countries to the world's four poorest nations.

Here is how you might tackle the first heading – Progress towards Millennium Development Goal 1.

You need to make and justify a conclusion about this progress.

Read all the sources and as you go underline/highlight the information that will help you make a conclusion about progress towards MDG1.

You will find MDG1 specified in source 1: reduce child mortality.

The evidence about progress towards reducing child mortality is found in source 3. It shows that there has been progress in reducing child mortality in the countries mentioned in the source.

So here is what you might write down as your answer:

The first conclusion is that there has been progress towards MDG1: reducing child mortality.

The evidence for this is found in source 3. The child mortality rate in Burundi has stayed the same from 1996 to 2006 but in the other countries it has been reduced. In Malawi the child mortality rate in 1996 was 216 per 1000 births and by 2006 it was 175 per 1000.

The same procedure should be used to deal with all four headings.

Marking

This is an 8-mark question. Up to 2 marks can be awarded for a valid conclusion with good justification. Four conclusions with justification are needed. Make sure you use all sources.

Now complete this answer yourself.

For you to do

Using the SQA Past Papers, find some more similar conclusion questions at Credit level. Answer these and check your answer with the answer section in the Past Papers. Ask your teacher to check them over.

EXPRESS SUPPORT FOR A GIVEN POINT OF VIEW

Arguments for and against (General Paper)

This type of Enquiry Skills question requires you to use the information in the sources to either support or reject a point of view. You can also be asked to give arguments for and/or against a viewpoint and to give reasons to support your view.

QUESTION 3 (C) (CONTINUED)

(b)   Study Sources 1 and 2 below, then answer the question which follows.

SOURCE 1

Information about selected countries		
Country	Average Income ($)	Life Expectancy (Years)
China	1,290	72
India	620	64
Russia	3,410	65
United Kingdom	33,940	79
United States	41,400	78

SOURCE 2

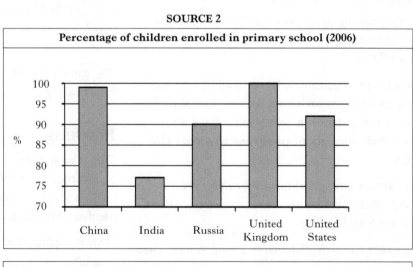

Percentage of children enrolled in primary school (2006)

China enrolls more of its children in primary school than most other major countries. People in China also have both the second lowest average income and shortest life expectancy.

View of An Qi

Using **only** Source 1 and Source 2 above, give **one** reason to **support** and **one** reason to **oppose** the view of An Qi.

(Enquiry Skills, **4** marks)

Answering the question

'BUS' the question

Using **only** Source 1 and Source 2 above, give **one** reason to **support** and **one** reason to **oppose** the view of An Qi.

This is a General Paper Enquiry Skills question worth 4 marks.

You can get up to 2 marks for each piece of evidence from the sources. You need two pieces of evidence – one to support part of An Qi's view and one to oppose part of the view. You need to make an obvious link between the view and the source.

The following sample answer would receive full marks:

Support the view:

An Qi says: 'China enrols more of its children in primary school than most other major countries.'

Evidence to support this view: This is true because source 2 shows that in China almost 100% of children were enrolled in primary school compared to other countries such as India (77%), Russia (90%) and the USA (92%). Only UK enrolled more of its children (100%).

Oppose the view:

An Qi says: 'People in China also have both the second lowest average income and shortest life expectancy.' (Note: this statement has two parts for you to deal with.)

Evidence to oppose this view: This is not true because source 1 shows that although China does have the second lowest average income, it does not have the shortest life expectancy. India (64years) and Russia (65 years) have a shorter life expectancy than China (72 years).

This answer is worth 4 out of 4 because:

- it answered the question set by giving one reason to support and one reason to oppose a view
- all sources were used
- the statistics were used correctly
- the answer was structured.

For you to do

Using the SQA Past Papers, find some more for/against type questions at General level. Answer these and check your answer with the answer section in the Past Papers. Ask your teacher to check them over.

EXPRESS SUPPORT FOR OR OPPOSITION TO A POINT OF VIEW (CREDIT PAPER)

QUESTION 1 (CONTINUED)

(c)   Study the Background Information about Gleninch and Sources 1 and 2 on the next page, then answer the question which follows.

BACKGROUND INFORMATION ABOUT GLENINCH CONSTITUENCY

- Gleninch is a constituency in the north of Scotland with a population of 35 265 people. It is a largely rural area with only one town, Inverinch, and a large number of scattered villages. The traditional industries of farming and fishing have been in decline in recent years. The unemployment rate is well above the national average.
- Many young people leave the area, moving to the big cities throughout the UK to look for jobs or to attend college or university.
- Tourism is very important to the local economy, with a lot of people employed in hotels, bed and breakfast accommodation and restaurants. Tourists tend to visit the area for a few days on short breaks, attracted by rare wildlife and spectacular, unspoilt scenery. However, there are a number of transport problems in the constituency, including high petrol prices and poor public transport.
- There is a proposal to build a wind farm in the area. This would involve the construction of 6 large wind turbines along the coast, as well as a 15-mile long power line built on tall pylons to take electricity to the rest of the country. This would create a few temporary construction jobs but will disturb local wildlife and impact on the scenery of the area.
- An American mining company wants to build a huge "super-quarry" into a mountainside near Gleninch. This will produce crushed rock to build roads, railways and houses throughout the UK. The new quarry will create 150 new jobs in Gleninch.
- At the last General Election, the constituency was won by the Labour Party with a majority of just over 1000 votes. The Liberal Democrats came second. They are convinced that, with the right candidate, they can win the seat at the next election.

A Statistical Profile of Gleninch Constituency (2006)

	Gleninch	Comparison with Scottish Average
Average Income	£21 185	−14%
Income Support claimants	15·1%	+22%
Unemployment Rate	5·6%	+13%
School leavers with no qualifications	3·6%	−33%
School leavers with Highers	58·6%	+13%
Serious Assaults	8·8 (per 10 000 people)	−73%
Housebreaking	3·8 (per 10 000 people)	−93%
Road Accidents	57 casualties	−44%

Survey of Local Liberal Democrat Members

Question: *How important are these issues to people in the area?*

Issue	Unimportant	Not Very Important	Fairly Important	Very Important
Environment	5%	25%	40%	30%
Health	2%	10%	53%	35%
Jobs	0%	0%	48%	52%
Women in Parliament	15%	52%	22%	11%

QUESTION 1 (*c*) (CONTINUED)

There are two people hoping to be selected by the Liberal Democratic Party to be the Party's candidate at the next General Election. Here are extracts from speeches they have made.

SOURCE 1

EXTRACT FROM CAMPAIGN SPEECH BY KIRSTY REID

- I support the proposed wind farm as it will provide many local jobs and help the local environment.
- Our local schools provide an excellent education. If selected, I will work to ensure this continues.
- Women make up over half the country's population and yet there are still very few of us who are MPs. This is a major priority for local party members and is an important reason why I should be the candidate.
- The local economy has been in decline recently. We need more jobs to keep our young people in the area. The new quarry will help with this, and I will work hard to see that it is allowed to go ahead.
- To attract more people to the area we need to improve transport links. I will make this a priority.

SOURCE 2

EXTRACT FROM CAMPAIGN SPEECH BY ROBBIE McKAY

- Tourism is very important to the area and so I will oppose the new wind farm as it will be an ugly blot on the landscape and deter tourists.
- Crime in Gleninch is among the worst in Scotland. I will campaign to improve policing in the area.
- Although new jobs are important, local Liberal Democrats are much more concerned about the environment. The new quarry will put more heavy lorries on our roads which are already more dangerous than the rest of the country. I will oppose it going ahead.
- The issue of health will be one of my main concerns, just as it is for local party members.
- Compared to the rest of the country, the people of Gleninch are not well-off. I will do all I can to improve this.

Use **only** the information about Gleninch on *Page four* and Sources 1 and 2 above.

(i) State **which person** would be the **more suitable** to be selected by the Liberal Democratic Party as their candidate for this constituency at the next General Election.

(ii) Give **three detailed reasons to support your choice**.

(iii) Give **two detailed** reasons why you **rejected** the other candidate.

In your answer, you **must relate** information about the constituency to the information about the **two** candidates.

(Enquiry Skills, **10** marks)

Answering the question

In this question, you are asked to make a recommendation (say which candidate is more suitable), provide three reasons to support that recommendation, as well as two reasons for rejecting the alternative.

The question is worth 10 marks altogether. Read the actual question first. You will always find the question after the sources.

'BUS' the question

Use **only** the information about Gleninch and Sources 1 and 2 above.

(i) State **which person** would be the **more suitable** to be selected by the Liberal Democratic Party as their candidate for this constituency at the next General Election.

(ii) Give **three detailed reasons** to support your choice.

(iii) Give **two detailed reasons** why you rejected the other candidate.

In your answer, you **must relate** information about the constituency to the information about the **two** candidates.

Since the question is worth 10 marks you might need about 12–15 minutes to answer it. There is a lot of reading to do but this can be made easier if you use a strategy, such as knowing how the marks are allocated, as demonstrated in the following example.

You have to choose one person (from two) as candidate for the Liberal Democrats in Gleninch Constituency.

You will get no marks for only writing the name of one of the candidates.

You have to give three detailed reasons why you have chosen that candidate. For each reason you can get up to 2 marks.

You must also make explicit (obvious) links between your candidate's campaign speech and the other candidate's speech and the information about Gleninch constituency (given in the Background information box).

If you do not make explicit links you will get no marks.

You also have to give two detailed reasons why you did not choose the other person. Again, you need to make explicit links between the candidate's speech and the other candidate's speech and the background information on Gleninch.

Up to 2 marks can be given for detailed reasons about why you rejected this candidate.

Here is part of an answer to this question:

(i) I have chosen Kirsty Reid to be the more suitable candidate to be selected by the Liberal Democrats to stand in Gleninch constituency.

(ii) The first reason is that the statistical profile of Gleninch shows that school leavers with Highers is 58.6% which is 13% above the Scottish average. Kirsty says (source 1) that she will ensure that the local schools continue to provide an excellent education. Robbie McKay, on the other hand, does not mention education in his campaign speech.

The second reason is that an American mining company wants to build a super quarry that will create 150 new jobs in Gleninch. Kirsty says that she will work hard to make sure that this quarry goes ahead since traditional industries such as farming and forestry have recently been in decline. The unemployment rate in Gleninch is also 13% above the national average.

The third reason is... *(do this yourself following the format above).*

(iii) I have rejected Robbie McKay because of the following two reasons.

The first reason is that he says in his speech that crime in Gleninch is among the worst in Scotland but the information about Gleninch shows that crime is actually quite low. Serious assaults are 73% lower than the Scottish average and house breakings are 93% lower. So obviously Robbie has not done his research properly.

The second reason is that the local Liberal Democrats are concerned about the environment (70%) but are more concerned about bringing jobs to Gleninch (100%). Robbie McKay opposes the new quarry despite the fact it will bring 150 new jobs to the area.

For you to do

Using the SQA Past Papers, find some more examples of this type of question at Credit level. Answer these and check your answer with the answer section of the Past Papers. Ask your teacher to check them over.

INVESTIGATING-TYPE QUESTIONS

These are also called Enquiry Skills questions in the exam paper. Look at the end of the question to see if the question is Knowledge and Understanding or Enquiry Skills.

You can easily recognise investigating-type questions because they have a distinctive logo beside them. It is a head with a question mark in it.

Types of investigating questions

These questions require you to use your own knowledge.

General level

There are basically two types of investigating questions at General level:

- giving aims relevant to an investigation
- justifying an enquiry method and stating any advantages/disadvantages of an enquiry method.

Credit level

There are three main types of investigating questions at Credit level:

- making up an appropriate hypothesis
- giving aims relevant to an investigation
- justifying an enquiry method and stating any advantages/disadvantages of an enquiry method.

GIVING AIMS IN RELATION TO AN INVESTIGATION (GENERAL AND CREDIT)

Aims

Aims are the key things you want to get answers to in your investigation.

They could start with the phrases:

- To find out about …
- To research …
- To compare …

When making up aims for the investigation on voting in the UK, you need to:

- make sure that your aim is linked directly to what you are investigating, that is, voting in the UK
- make sure that your aim is worded appropriately.

In your aim you should include the following ideas (but only if relevant):

- social factors
- economic factors
- political factors.

Also include Modern Studies concepts where appropriate, such as:

- representation
- rights and responsibilities
- participation
- ideology
- power
- need
- equality.

Your investigation

In this example, you are investigating the topic of 'Voting in the UK.'

> VOTING IN THE UK
>
> As part of the **Planning Stage**, give **two** relevant **aims** for your investigation.
>
> (Enquiry Skills, 2 marks)

You have to give two relevant aims.

Think about what you studied when you looked at the topic 'Voting in the UK'. You would have looked at the concepts of representation, rights and responsibilities and participation. You would have studied what systems of voting we use, i.e. FPTP and AMS. You will know about the Scottish Parliament and the UK Parliament and MPs, MSPs. You should try to bring this sort of knowledge into your aim.

So a sample answer to the question would be:

Two relevant aims for voting in the UK would be:

- *To find out the different ways of voting in the UK*
- *To find out what voting system people prefer.*

These aims would get 1 mark each, so the answer would receive the full 2 marks.

For you to do

- Make up another two aims for this investigation 'Voting in the UK'.
- Using the SQA Past Papers, look for and answer this type of question. Check your answers with your teacher.

STATE AND JUSTIFY AN ENQUIRY METHOD

> Give **two** ways in which you could contact the political parties.
>
> For **each** way you have chosen, explain why it is a **good** way to get information to help in your investigation.
>
> (Enquiry Skills, **4** marks)
>
> You decide to use your local library to help with your investigation.
>
> Describe **one** way in which you could use your local library.
>
> (Enquiry Skills, **2** marks)

'BUS' the question

> Give **two** ways in which you could contact the political parties.
>
> For **each** way you have chosen, explain why it is a **good** way to get information to help in your investigation.

The question asks you to give two ways in which you could contact the political parties; then for each way you must explain why it is a good way to get information you need to help you with your investigation (which is campaigning in elections).

Marking

You will get 1 mark for each correct way/method.

You will also get 1 mark for each correct reason/advantage of choosing that method.

The following answer would receive full (4/4) marks:

One good way to contact the political parties to get information for the investigation on campaigning in elections would be to send the parties an email. This is a good way because you can have a number of detailed questions that you would like answered by all the parties and they would get the email quickly and hopefully they would reply quickly.

Another way would be to telephone the local party offices. This is a good way to get information because you can speak to the person most likely to help you and get an answer to your questions quickly.

Describe **one** way in which you could use your local library.

This part of the question asks you about using the local library to help you with your investigation. You have to describe one way in which you could use your local library (2 marks). To get the 2 marks you will need some detail.

An answer would receive full (2/2) marks if it included two of the following points:

- Lots of books and magazines and other publications that you can borrow and read to get the information about your topic.

- Expert advice from librarians who are trained to help you find information.

- Most local libraries have free access to the internet which you could use to search the internet or send emails.

For you to do

Using the SQA Past Papers, look for and answer this type of question. Check your answers with your teacher.

MAKING UP A RELEVANT HYPOTHESIS (CREDIT PAPER)

Read carefully the information about investigating-type questions given in the General level section (pages 108–111). The information about aims and methods is the same for Credit questions.

There are a couple of differences, however. Firstly, note that the question may say **in detail**. This means that you have to give more than just the basic answer. You should try to give a point and then expand on it. (PEEC it!) Secondly, the first question is normally asking you to state a relevant hypothesis for your investigation.

A **hypothesis**:

● is an educated guess at what you might find out if you were to carry out the investigation
● requires your detailed knowledge of the topic
● is always a statement and never a question
● is always relevant to the title of the investigation
● is developed (to get 2 marks)
● should contain some **biased** words such as all, none.

> all   none   most   everyone   no-one   nothing   only

Try to include some of the following, if appropriate:

● social factors
● economic factors
● political factors.

Also mention Modern Studies concepts when relevant:

● representation
● rights and responsibilities
● participation
● ideology
● need
● equality
● power.

QUESTION 2 (CONTINUED)

You have been asked to carry out an investigation on the topic in the box below.

> **Help for families in the UK**

Now answer questions (*b*), (*c*), (*d*) and (*e*) which follow

(*b*)   State a relevant **hypothesis** for your investigation.

(Enquiry Skills, **2** marks)

(*c*)   Give **two** relevant **aims** to help you prove or disprove your hypothesis.

(Enquiry Skills, **2** marks)

Your Modern Studies class decides to use **Video Conferencing** to do an interview to help the pupils with their investigations into "**Help for families in the UK**".

Your teacher contacted your MP at Westminster, who said she would be willing to be interviewed. The interview set up is shown below.

| Your MP in her office at Westminster | A secondary school classroom |

(*d*)   Give **two relevant** questions which you could ask your MP to help with your investigation.

(Enquiry Skills, **4** marks)

[Turn over

QUESTION 2 (CONTINUED)

While collecting information for your investigation, you found the **Orinoco Web page** below which contained information about **Social Trends 2008**.

orinoco.co.uk   🛒 VIEW BASKET | WISH LIST | YOUR ACCOUNT | HELP

WELCOME | YOUR STORE | BOOKS | ELECTRONICS & PHOTO | MUSIC | DVD BUY & RENT | VIDEO | SOFTWARE | PC & VIDEO GAMES | HOME & GARDEN | TOYS & GAMES | SPORTS & LEISURE | JEWELLERY & WATCHES

Search   Books ▼   GO!

Social Trends (Paperback)
by Office for National Statistics (Author)

Our Price: £45.00

Availability: Not in stock.
              Pay now, delivered in 2 months.

Price: £45.00
out of stock
Dispatched from and sold by
Orinoco.co.uk
Quantity: 1 ▼
🛒 Add to Shopping Basket
or
Sign in to turn on 1-Click ordering.

More Buying Choices

See larger image
Share your own customer images

Social Trends 2008—book description

A reference source of 252 pages, "**Social Trends 2008**" draws together social and economic data from a range of government departments and other organisations. Social Trends has been published every year since 1970 by the Office for National Statistics. This annual publication provides a picture of life and lifestyle in the UK. Data is presented in a combination of tables, figures and text.

(*e*)   Using **only** the Orinoco Web page, give one **disadvantage** of **buying** from this website and one **advantage** of **using** Social Trends 2008 in your investigation.

(Enquiry Skills, **2** marks)

Investigation

> State a relevant **hypothesis** for your investigation.

You must now state a relevant hypothesis. You are investigating the topic 'Help for families in the UK.' What might your hypothesis be?

Think about your knowledge of the topic 'Help for families in the UK.' You will know about financial benefits from the UK government such as child benefit. You will know about other financial benefits such as child tax credit. What about other help from voluntary organisations such as Gingerbread?

The following hypothesis would be awarded 2 marks:

Child benefit should only be given to families who really need it.

This hypothesis would receive 2 marks because:

● it relates directly to the topic being investigated
● it specifically mentions help that a family can get, that is, child benefit

- it shows you know that child benefit is currently given to all families and you are questioning whether it should be means tested or not
- it contains some exaggerated words: Child benefit should <u>only</u> be given to families who <u>really</u> need it
- it contains a relevant Modern Studies concept: need.

> Give **two** relevant aims to help you prove or disprove your hypothesis.

All of the information provided in the section about aims in the General paper is relevant at Credit as well. The main difference is that you need more depth.

For example, for the hypothesis 'Child benefit should <u>only</u> be given to families who <u>really</u> need it' two aims that you could identify would be:

- To find out whether different families think child benefit should be means tested or not
- To find out the extent to which child benefit helps meet the financial needs of families.

These aims would receive 1 mark each.

> Give **two** relevant questions which you could ask your MP to help with your investigation.

This question takes the investigation a step further in that you have to make up two relevant questions you would want to ask your local MP to help your investigation into child benefit and helping families. The video conferencing is just the same as asking the MP face-to-face.

You can get 2 marks for a question if it is detailed and linked directly to your investigation about child benefit and families. Some 2-mark questions are:

- What kind of social and financial problems do families contact you with?
- What does the UK parliament do to help some lone-parent families cope with their financial problems?

Questions like these might just get you 1 mark:

- Do you help families?
- How much is child benefit today?

> Using **only** the Orinoco Web page, give one disadvantage of buying from this website and one advantage of using Social Trends 2008 in your investigation.

In this question you have to state what is bad about buying from a particular website and then say what is good about using a certain book to help you with your investigation. This should be an easy way to get 2 marks.

Look carefully at the Orinoco web page. An obvious disadvantage is that the book you want is out of stock and you won't be able to get a copy for two months. By the time you get the book it will be too late for you. Another disadvantage might be that the book costs £45. This is expensive and it's possible that your school can't afford to buy a book at that price for just one pupil. (1 mark)

You want to buy the book *Social Trends 2008*. There are many advantages of using this book in your investigation. Look carefully at the web page to identify some of the advantages, for example:

It is the 2008 version of the book and since this is the latest edition it means it will have very up-to-date statistics and tables. (1 mark)

For you to do

- Make up some more hypotheses for this investigation. Discuss them with your teacher.
- Using the SQA Past Papers, look for and complete questions on hypotheses.
- Make up some investigation titles of your own. Then make up a selection of relevant hypotheses.

METHODS OF ENQUIRY

Part of the Enquiry Skills investigating-type questions might be about the advantages and/or disadvantages of certain methods of enquiry.

The methods of enquiry you could be asked about are:

- interrogation of a database/data file
- the internet
- questionnaires
- attitude surveys
- structured interviews
- structured letters
- structured observations
- fieldwork
- library research (using books, periodicals, CD-ROMs)
- media interrogations (TV, radio, newspapers)
- using statistical information.

INTERROGATION OF A DATABASE/DATA FILE

A database or data file is a huge collection of information, often in the form of statistics. It is normally on a CD-ROM or on the internet. For example, a police force will have databases about crime in their area.

Factors to consider when using a database/data file

- You need to know what search words you want to type in to the search box.
- Is the data file up to date?

Advantages include:

- lots of information can be obtained quickly
- information is usually in a table
- information is normally statistical
- information can be printed or viewed on screen.

Disadvantages include:

- you can only get information that has been put on the database
- statistics may not be correct
- the results you get will need to be analysed
- it can be time consuming.

THE INTERNET

Factors to consider when using the internet

- Use a search engine that you know is reliable.
- Be specific with your searches; key words are important.
- Save materials once you have accessed them, this saves working on line all of the time.

Advantages include:

- it can be accessed at any time
- it provides up-to-date information that is often not readily available from any other source, e.g. international newspapers
- it provides links to similar sites
- you can get the information quickly.

Disadvantages include:

- you need a computer with a modem and broadband connection that is fast otherwise it can take a long time to download information and so costs more money
- it's not always possible to find the source of the information
- the information can be biased
- it can give you too much information, making it hard to find exactly what you are looking for.

QUESTIONNAIRES

Questionnaires are lists of questions you are going to ask so you can collect information. Questions can be open (e.g. What do you think about ...?) or closed (e.g. Did you vote in the last election?). Open questions allow more expanded answers whereas closed questions normally get a one-word answer.

Factors to consider when using questionnaires

- Make sure your questions are written so that you can get the appropriate answers.

- Choose an appropriate random sample, e.g. a minimum of 100, and a variety of respondents (different ages, both males and females, different ethnic/cultural background).

Advantages include:

- it is easy to get people to answer questionnaires
- appropriate questions can be asked
- it is quite cheap to carry out.

Disadvantages include:

- it can take you a long time to analyse the results
- you need to get a large number of people to answer the questionnaire (a minimum of 100) for a valid result
- you need to ask the sample within a short space of time to get reliable results
- closed questions can limit what people think so you do not get a true response.

ATTITUDE SURVEYS

An attitude survey is a way of finding out people's thoughts and opinions on a matter.

Factors to consider when using an attitude survey

You need to be very clear what the survey is trying to find out so the questions can be focussed.

Advantages include:

- you can get opinions and thoughts on issues (more in-depth than in questionnaires)
- it is good for personal issues like capital punishment.

Disadvantages include:

- you need to make sure questions are worded appropriately
- it is more difficult to analyse answers compared with questionnaires
- people often do not fill in the surveys and do not send them back.

STRUCTURED INTERVIEWS

A structured interview is when you have planned a set of questions to ask a person or group at a set time. You plan the interview in advance.

Factors to consider when using structured interviews

- It may be useful to ask if you can tape the interview so you can spend time afterwards understanding the answers.
- The person you are interviewing will probably be an expert so you will need to be well prepared.

Advantages include:

- it will usually be a face-to-face interview with an expert so you can get good information
- it allows you to add extra questions depending on what the interviewee says
- if you do not understand something you can ask the person to explain the point.

Disadvantages include:

- an expert can give you too much information and you can get bogged down in information not immediately relevant to your enquiry
- it can take up lots of your time
- you can make inaccurate notes because you are misinterpreting the answers.

STRUCTURED LETTERS

A structured letter will ask specific questions to help you with your investigation.

Factors to consider when using structured letters

- Address the letter accurately.
- Say who you are and where you are from, describe the purpose of your enquiry, and always thank the person.

Advantages include:

- you can duplicate the letter if you use a word processor, so you can send many letters out at a time
- you can send letters directly to the appropriate people.

Disadvantages include:

- the person may not reply or you may get a standard letter that gives you inappropriate information
- you might get useless information back such as leaflets.

STRUCTURED OBSERVATIONS

A structured observation is one that you plan in advance. You might make up a checklist of things for you to look out for when you observe.

Factors to consider when using structured observations

Arrangements must be made well in advance if the visit is to be useful. Remember that what you see or find out might be biased.

Advantages include:

- it is good to see things at first hand, and you are more likely to remember them
- you can often arrange a time that suits you
- you can take a camera and/or tape recorder to record your observations.

Disadvantages include:

- it may be difficult to analyse your results
- you may not get the whole truth
- people may not like being observed.

FIELDWORK

Fieldwork is done outside the classroom, visiting places or people where you can collect data and information.

Factors to consider when undertaking fieldwork

- If you are going on a visit, for example to a sheltered housing complex, make sure you are well organised: arrange visit in advance; prepare questions, etc.
- Make sure your questions make sense. They should be a mixture of open and closed questions.

Advantages include:

- you will be able to ask questions face to face with the interviewee
- you can get a feel for the place you are visiting
- you will remember the visit and be able to add extra information to your investigation.

Disadvantages include:

- you might not be allowed to go on the visit
- you might not get to see what you want to see nor speak to the person you want to speak to
- you might get too much irrelevant information.

LIBRARY RESEARCH

Libraries don't have only books. They also have newspapers, journals, periodicals, CD-ROMs, etc. You will need to know the advantages of using different items in a library.

Factors to consider when undertaking library research

- Make sure you are a member of the library, even the school library.
- Know how to use the computer to find out where the book/periodical is kept.

Advantages include:

- there will be a good range of information available, e.g. books, magazines, newspapers, CD-ROMs, etc.
- it will be easy to access since every school/town has a library
- it is free
- back copies are often available.

Disadvantages include:

- libraries can provide too much material
- books you want may not be available
- books may be out of date
- the library is not always open.

MEDIA INTERROGATION

You need to know about the different types of media, e.g. TV, radio, newspapers, videos, DVDs, etc.

Factors to consider when undertaking a media interrogation

- When watching videos, watch the programme twice.
- Make sure the item is up to date, especially videos.

Advantages include:

- the material is cheap and easy to get
- TV generally provides up-to-date information
- news programmes are usually not biased
- if you have satellite or cable TV you can get foreign news.

Disadvantages include:

- newspapers are usually biased
- the material may be inaccurate, e.g. TV news stories are one person's interpretation of a story
- videos and DVDs can be out of date.

USING STATISTICAL INFORMATION

Factors to consider when using statistical information

- The statistics should be reliable and valid (and up to date).
- You should be able to understand them.

Advantages include:

- you should be able to draw suitable conclusions from the statistics
- check they are up to date.

Disadvantages include:

- statistics can be difficult to understand
- statistics can be misinterpreted.